STEP-BY-STEP

Word
for
Windows 6.0

STEP-BY-STEP

Word
for
Windows 6.0

Sue Nugus and Steve Harris

NEW·TECH

Newtech
An Imprint of Butterworth-Heinemann Ltd
Linacre House, Jordan Hill, Oxford OX2 8DP

 A member of the Reed Elsevier plc Group

OXFORD   LONDON   BOSTON
MUNICH   NEW DELHI   SINGAPORE   SYDNEY
TOKYO   TORONTO   WELLINGTON
First published 1994
© Sue Nugus and Steve Harris 1994

NOTICE
The authors and the publisher have used their best efforts to prepare this book, including the computer examples contained in it. The computer examples have all been tested. The authors and the publisher make no warranty, implicit or explicit, about the documentation. The authors and the publisher will not be liable under any circumstances for any direct or indirect damages arising from any use, direct or indirect, of the documentation or computer examples contained in this book.

TRADEMARKS/REGISTERED TRADEMARKS
Computer hardware and software brand names mentioned in this book are protected by their respective trademarks and are acknowledged.

British Library Cataloguing in Publication Data
A catalogue record for this book is available from the British Library.

ISBN 0 7506 1813 2

Typeset by TechTrans Ltd, Reading.

Printed and bound in Great Britain.

Contents

ONE
Getting Ready

Key Learning Points in This Chapter

- An introduction to Word
- New features in Word 6
- Hardware and software requirements
- An overview of DOS
- Windows fundamentals
- Windows applications
- Installing Word

Background to Word

Microsoft have had a brief, but successful history. From supplying the operating system to IBM for the PC, they have become one of the most successful software companies in the world.

From that small start, they have grown and grown, not only producing the industry standard operating systems and environments such as MS-DOS and Windows, but also producing a range of applications that are difficult to fault.

Word was one of the first large-scale applications to be released by Microsoft during their expansion. Initially available as a DOS-based program it competed with long-term favourites such as WordPerfect and WordStar. In its early days it was not as popular as its developers would have liked, offering little that was not available elsewhere.

However, with the advent of Windows, Word started to become more popular, rapidly overtaking the older DOS-based software in terms of new sales and general popularity. This was no real surprise, as the Windows environment made Word much easier to use, especially with a mouse, and much more graphically appealing with WYSIWYG fonts and graphics.

Microsoft Office

Of course Word is not the only Microsoft application. An entire suite of complementary products is available offering a spreadsheet, graphics, project management, interpersonal mail and many other features beside. This group of applications is known as the Microsoft Office, and can be purchased as a bundled set or as individual packages.

The great thing about all of these programs is that they work in much the same way, and so after having learnt to use Word you'll find that you can master other products in the set in about half the time it might otherwise take.

Of course there are other benefits as well, including easy transfer of information from one application to another, automated use of the mail system through any of the applications and so on.

Other books in this "step-by-step" series have been written to show you how
to make the most of Excel 5 and the other Microsoft Office applications.

New Features in Word for Windows 6.0

Word has been seen as one of the flagship products from Microsoft, offering
an easy to use, attractive and productive environment for word processing.
However, until the release of Word for Windows 6.0 it had not been updated
for a number of years (with the exception of minor interim releases and
patches) so was occasionally criticised for lagging behind its competitors in
terms of the features and facilities it offered.

Word 6 has answered these criticisms with some aplomb, featuring many new
tools and options as well as updating and refining many of those that featured
in previous releases.

Why Word for Windows 6.0?

Microsoft Word has for some time been acknowledged as one of the most
popular word processors for the Windows operating environment. In addition,
Microsoft Word has been available to users of the Apple Macintosh computer
for a number of years, and has become equally popular. These two different
versions have shared a lot of features, with common tools and menu options
being the most obvious. However, under the surface there were some
fundamental differences, one of the most noticeable being the different file
formats used for each system.

Version 6.0 has eliminated most of these differences, with both Word for
Windows and Word for the Macintosh sharing the same file format, features,
appearance and documentation. Thus it was a natural step to align the version
numbers so that they would correspond, making it immediately obvious to
users of each system that they can now work together much more easily.

Intellisense

Word has an automatic correction feature known as Intellisense. As you type
at the keyboard, Intellisense checks what you are entering for any common
errors and corrects them if it can. For example, if you type in "teh" instead

of "the" then Intellisense will correct the word automatically. It can also correct other common mistakes such as capitalising the first two letters of a word rather than just the first (e.g. MEmorandum), capitalising the first letter of a sentence etc.

Of course Intellisense can be switched on/off and customised as necessary, so a list of common personal typing mistakes can be maintained, giving the user total control of this powerful facility.

Another important use of this facility is as a shorthand aid for common terms. For example, if you tend to use the word "correspondence" frequently, Intellisense could be configured to recognise "corr" and replace it with "correspondence", thereby minimising typing time.

Toolbars

Word now supports customised, floating toolbars, in a similar way to Microsoft Excel. This means that a greater variety of toolbars and icons are available as standard, and in addition personal toolbars can be created as necessary.

The standard toolbars are context sensitive, so when you are working in outline view the outlining toolbar is displayed, when in Print Preview mode the Print Preview toolbar is displayed and so on.

Custom toolbars can be created very easily, and allow buttons and icons to be used to represent macros and other commands.

Advanced Formatting Options

Another major advance for Word is the provision of a variety of professionally designed document formats, any one of which can be applied with a few clicks of the mouse. This allows users with little or no previous experience of Word or any other WYSIWYG (What You See Is What You Get) word processor to quickly and easily produce high-quality, professional-looking documentation.

Many of the formatting features will be introduced and discussed throughout this book.

What You Need to Have

In order to work so hard for you, Word has some fairly stringent hardware and software requirements. These must be met before you can install and use the software.

Minimum Hardware Requirements

Like other Windows software, Word requires a powerful PC and plenty of storage. The following table summarises the requirements, showing both the minimum and recommended specifications:

	Minimum	Recommended
PC Processor Memory	80286 4MB	80486 at 33MHz 8MB or more
Free disk space	8MB	18MB
Floppy disk drive	3½" or 5¼" high density	3½" or 5¼" high density
Video adapter	EGA or above	VGA or above

Note that the brand names of the PC and any peripherals are largely irrelevant – any system that is compatible with the Microsoft Windows environment should be suitable.

Printers

Word is capable of producing very high quality output, comprised of a combination of text and graphics. However, for this to print satisfactorily it will be necessary to have a high-quality laser printer or similar. The two most popular laser printer "families" are PostScript printers and HP LaserJet printers (and their compatibles).

PostScript printers tend to be the most flexible, offering a number of in-built fonts and graphical effects. They are typically equipped with 2MB of more of memory, and have their own on-board processor and so are ideally suited to Windows applications such as Word.

HP LaserJet printers, and especially the compatibles, tend to be less expensive. Ideally they need to be equipped with at least 2MB of printer memory to allow them to print the graphics that Word can produce.

A good compromise may be to buy a LaserJet (or compatible) printer that can later be upgraded by the addition of a PostScript cartridge. If this approach is taken then it is recommended that only a good brand-name printer is chosen (such as a true Hewlett-Packard) as this will minimise compatibility problems.

Software

In addition to the hardware requirements there is also a need to have a certain level of software installed prior to Word.

Firstly, the operating system should be either DOS 5 or DOS 6.X. Proprietary versions from the manufacturer of the PC (such as Compaq, IBM, Toshiba) are fine as long as they are the right numeric version. You can check this be typing VER at the DOS command prompt. A message similar to the following should be produced:

```
C:\WINDOWS>ver

MS-DOS Version 5.00
```

In addition to the operating system, it is necessary to have Microsoft Windows installed. The minimum version that is required is Windows 3.1. Windows for Workgroups 3.1 or 3.11 will also work without problems, also providing mail facilities for communicating and transferring data to other users.

To check which version of Windows is installed, choose *Help*, *About Program Manager* from the main Windows desktop. Figure 1.1 shows the dialogue box that will be displayed:

This book assumes that DOS and Windows have already been installed onto the PC. If not, consult the documentation that was supplied and carefully follow the installation guidelines.

Figure 1.1.
Finding the
version number.

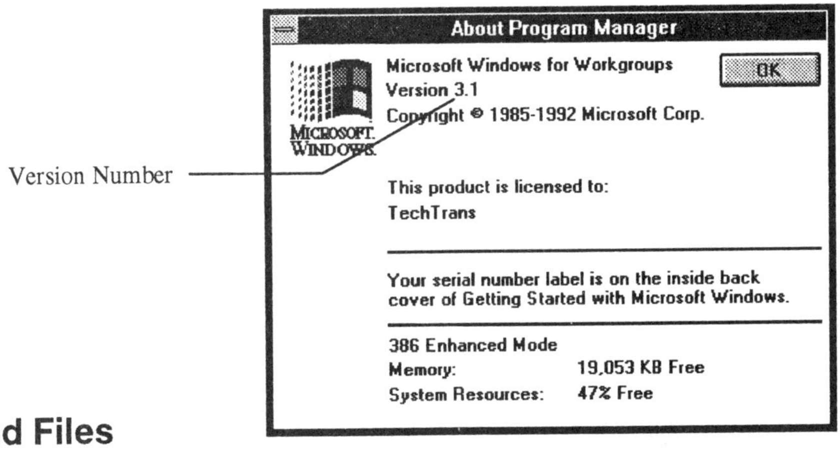

Version Number ——————

DOS, Directories and Files

In order to efficiently manage the information on your PC, it will be necessary to know a little about the operating system – DOS. This is the underlying piece of software that allows you to run programs such as Word, but it is also responsible for ensuring that your documents and information are stored correctly. In effect it is your filing system.

DOS works on the basis of textual commands which you type in from the keyboard when you want DOS to do something. These commands bear some similarity to English; for example, COPY duplicates information, ERASE removes it and so on. Some of the most relevant commands are discussed below.

The majority of these commands relate to the storage and management of your information. This is stored in the form of separate files, groups of which can be managed in directories.

Files and Filenames

A DOS file is similar to a conventional paper-based file. It holds information in a logical order, it is referenced by name and it is stored somewhere, in this case on a disk rather than in a filing cabinet.

Files are created by your applications when you work with them. The process of creating a file is usually called Saving, whilst the process of retrieving an existing file is known as *Opening* or *Loading*. When these operations are performed, it is necessary to specify a filename – an identifier that is used to uniquely locate the file.

DOS filenames are a little limited in terms of what is allowed. The standard format for a filename restricts you to just 8 characters, with a further 3 optional characters being used by the software. The 8 character portion is simply known as the *filename*, whilst the 3 character portion is known as the *extension*. These two sections are separated by a ".". The following are examples of valid filenames:

> CORRESP.DOC   MYLETTER.TXT   SAMPLE.

Notice that the third example has no file extension – this is perfectly valid as the extension is optional. The extension is used to categorise the files into different types, so for example a DOC extension indicates that the file contains a Word document, whilst an extension of XLS signifies that the file contains an Excel spreadsheet.

Both the name and extension are restricted to using only certain characters, namely alphanumeric characters and some punctuation symbols. However, it is advisable to use only the following, to minimise any confusion:

> Letters   A–Z
> Numbers   0–9
> Underscore   _

The underscore character should be used where a space is required. It is also worth remembering that upper and lower case are considered to be the same, so MYFILE.DOC is the same as MyFile.Doc.

The following are examples of valid and invalid filenames:

Valid	Invalid
MEMO0194.DOC	SAMPLES93.DOC (Too many letters)
OLD_DATA.TXT	NOTES**.XLS (No * allowed)
FIRST.	TEL NUMS.LST (No spaces allowed)
Names.DOC	

Directories

All of the available files can be listed in a *directory*, which shows their names, extensions, sizes, and the date and time they were last modified. A typical directory listing may appear as follows:

```
Volume in drive C has no label
 Volume Serial Number is 1AD9-4D80
 Directory of C:\WIN

256COLOR BMP      5078 10-01-92    3:11a
AB       DLL     97584 10-01-92    3:11a
ACCESSOR GRP      6230 12-31-93    2:40p
APPLICAT GRP      5924 12-31-93    2:40p
ARCADE   BMP       630 10-01-92    3:11a
ARGYLE   BMP       630 10-01-92    3:11a
ARTGALRY INI        89 12-17-93   10:11a
BOOTLOG  TXT      2458 06-25-93   11:11a
CALC     EXE     43072 10-01-92    3:11a
CALC     HLP     18076 10-01-92    3:11a
CANYON   MID     33883 10-01-92    3:11a
CARDFILE HLP     24810 10-01-92    3:11a
```

Notice that in this example the files are sorted by their filename. If you display a list of files on your computer's disk then they may be sorted into a different order, if at all. The topic of sorting files is discussed in the DOS reference manuals.

The Directory Tree

As you can imagine, once a few files have been created, such a directory listing would become extremely long and difficult to read. To overcome this problem files can be grouped and stored in subdirectories. You can think of a subdirectory as being analogous to a drawer in a filing cabinet, with each file being the equivalent of a single document within that drawer. Unlike the filing cabinet however, subdirectories are hierarchical – that is they form a tree-like structure which is collectively known as the *directory tree*. Diagramatically the directory tree can be represented as shown below:

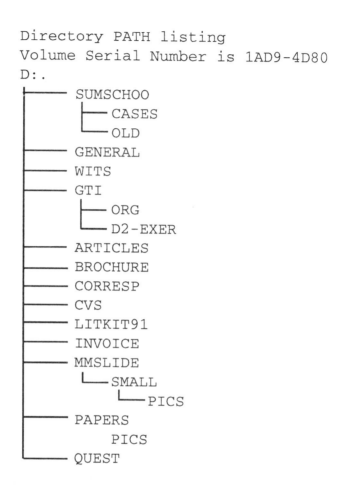

```
Directory PATH listing
Volume Serial Number is 1AD9-4D80
D:.
        ├────── SUMSCHOO
        │         ├── CASES
        │         └── OLD
        ├────── GENERAL
        ├────── WITS
        ├────── GTI
        │         ├── ORG
        │         └── D2-EXER
        ├────── ARTICLES
        ├────── BROCHURE
        ├────── CORRESP
        ├────── CVS
        ├────── LITKIT91
        ├────── INVOICE
        ├────── MMSLIDE
        │         └── SMALL
        │               └── PICS
        ├────── PAPERS
        │           PICS
        └────── QUEST
```

Notice that each subdirectory has a name, and this must obey the same rules as a standard filename. Note that it is quite possible for a subdirectory to have an extension as well as a name, although this is not usually included.

When viewing the contents of a subdirectory in the form of a directory listing, some differences will be apparent when compared with the simple directory listing shown previously.

The following is an extract from the full directory listing that corresponds to the directory tree shown above:

```
Volume in drive D has no label
 Volume Serial Number is 1AD9-4D80
 Directory of D:\DATA

.              <DIR>        07-09-93    9:45a
..             <DIR>        07-09-93    9:45a
GTI            <DIR>        07-09-93    9:46a
ARTICLES       <DIR>        07-09-93    9:46a
BPR            <DIR>        10-06-93    9:44a
BROCHURE       <DIR>        07-09-93    9:46a
CASEBOOK       <DIR>        07-09-93    9:48a
CORRESP        <DIR>        07-09-93    9:46a
CVS            <DIR>        07-09-93    9:46a
DAN            <DIR>        07-09-93    9:49a
DELPHI         <DIR>        07-09-93    9:47a
GENERAL        <DIR>        07-09-93    9:46a
GLOSSARY       <DIR>        08-24-93    9:41a
IMAGES         <DIR>        07-09-93    9:47a
INVOICE        <DIR>        07-09-93    9:46a
LITKIT91       <DIR>        07-09-93    9:46a
MMCONF94       <DIR>        07-26-93    4:46p
MMSLIDE        <DIR>        07-09-93    9:46a
PAPERS         <DIR>        07-09-93    9:47a
QUEST          <DIR>        07-09-93    9:48a
```

Notice that the top two entries are **.** and **..** – these are special entries that are used to move between the subdirectories. More will be seen about these entries later. Following the two special entries, the remainder of the listing consists of the names of the subdirectories. For example, the first subdirectory is called **GTI**, the second is called **ARTICLES** and so on. Notice that these correspond to the subdirectories shown in the graphical directory tree.

The first directory is known as the *root directory*,. Rather than having a name, the root directory is referenced using the "\" character. Furthermore, the root directory will be found to have no "." or ".." entries in its directory listing so it is a rather special case.

Disk Drives

Most computers are equipped with multiple disk drives, each of which is capable of storing a separate directory tree. Two types of disk drive may be encountered; floppy disk drives and hard disk drives.

Floppy disk drives allow different disks to be used on the PC, as the disk may be removed from the drive by opening the door. Hard disk drives are not removable, and are housed inside the PC. Because there is no need to make the disk accessible, hard disk drives operate at higher speeds, and are capable of storing greater amounts of information than floppy disk drives, and therefore are traditionally used as the main storage device. Floppy disks, due to their ability to be interchanged, are traditionally used for backups and for transferring information between computers.

When working with floppy disks make sure that you have read the guidelines for handling them and inserting them into the disk drives. These guidelines should have been supplied with your computer.

In order to differentiate between the different drives, alphabetic letters are used. Drive letters A and B are used to reference floppy disks, whilst drive letters C, D etc. are used to reference hard disks. Note that this scheme is used even on computers that have only a single floppy disk – A and B both refer to the same drive in this case.

Commands

DOS operates through the use of English-like commands. These are entered from the keyboard, and must be correctly spelt for them to be recognised. So that you will know when you can enter a command, DOS displays a prompt similar to the following:

```
D:\DATA\ARTICLES>
```

From this prompt you can see the current drive (D) and directory (\DATA\ARTICLES). This is the location where your command will take effect. For example, an ERASE command would erase some or all of the files in this location.

The appearance of the DOS prompt is a signal to you that the computer is waiting for you to enter a command, and the prompt will remain on screen until you do so. All of the available commands are discussed in the DOS manual that was provided with your PC, although one of the most important - Copy - is discussed in more detail below.

Copying Files

Files can be copied from one location to another using the COPY command. These locations could be different subdirectories, different drives or even different filenames within the same directory. It is up to you to specify this when you enter the command. The full *syntax* or layout of the command is:

```
COPY <Source File> <Destination File>
```

<Source File> refers to the name and location of the file to be copied, and <Destination File> tells DOS where you want to copy it to. Both source and destination can be specified as filenames, directory names, drive letters or any combination. Notice that there must be a space between the source and destination filenames.

For example, COPY LETTER1.DOC LETTER1.BAK copies the file called LETTER1.DOC to a new file called LETTER1.BAK, both of which will be in the current directory. However, COPY LETTER1.DOC A:\LETTER1.DOC copies the file to the root directory on disk A.

More information about the copy command can be found in the DOS reference manuals, but you should remember that it is not the only way to duplicate files. Windows is supplied with a utility to handle files called *File Manager*. This is discussed in the Windows reference manuals, and may be found to be easier to use for anyone already experienced with DOS.

Remember that you should regularly use File Manager or the DOS Copy command to make security backups of your files onto floppy disks, just in case the originals (usually on the hard disk) are damaged in some way.

Working with Directories

As mentioned, files are held within subdirectories on the disk. These are created and managed using three DOS commands MKDIR (or MD) to make a directory, CHDIR (or CD) to change to a different directory and RMDIR (or RD) to remove a directory.

For example, if you are currently working in a directory called DATA on the C drive (i.e. the DOS prompt shows `C:\DATA>`), a subdirectory called WPFILES could be created with:

```
MD WPFILES
```

If you wanted to then make the WPFILES directory current then you would use the following command:

```
CD WPFILES
```

At this stage the DOS prompt would read `C:\DATA\WPFILES>`. All commands issued would be executed in this directory, until you issued another CD command to move somewhere else. For example, to move back to the parent directory (C:\DATA) you would use either:

```
CD ..       or      CD \DATA
```

The WPFILES directory could then be removed with the RD command:

```
RD WPFILES
```

Note that it is *not* possible to remove a directory if it contains any files or subdirectories or if it is current (i.e. you are working in it).

Creating the STEPWORD Working Directory

The files created and used in the exercises throughout this book are assumed to be stored in a directory on the hard disk called STEPWORD. To create this directory :

1   Ensure you are in the root directory by typing **CD ** ENTER

2   Type **MD STEPWORD** ENTER

Running Windows

Perhaps the most important DOS command of all as far as we are concerned is the one that allows us to start Windows. This is done with the WIN command, which can be entered at any DOS prompt.

On entering the command, the screen should go blank for a few seconds and then display the Microsoft Windows Logo and copyright screen. After a few more seconds the main Windows display should appear. Obviously these timings are approximate and could vary quite substantially, especially on a slower computer system.

Windows Fundamentals

Windows provides a graphical user interface to allow you to work quickly and easily with the computer. This means that unlike DOS, commands are issued by pointing and clicking using the mouse, and information is displayed in graphical "windows".

The Desktop

The main working area is known as the *desktop*, and appears as shown in Figure 1.2. Note that the term "Desktop" refers to the entire shaded area – the section in the middle is called the Program Manager Window and is where you will be working from most of the time.

Figure 1.2.
The Windows
desktop.

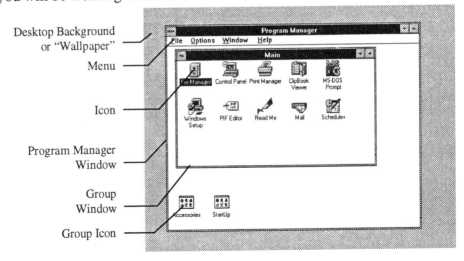

There are three main features that you can work with in Program Manager –icons, groups and menus. In addition, there are numerous other controls and features as we will see.

Icons

Icons are small images that represent individual programs or files. Activating an icon will run the program or load the data file as appropriate.

The actual image used for the icon usually gives some clue as to what the program will do. For example, a text editor may have a pen as its icon, whilst a drawing program may have a paintbrush and paint palette. There is also a short description of the icon shown beneath the image to give further information.

Groups

Groups contain icons. In many ways groups can be thought of as the Windows equivalent of a subdirectory, with the icons representing the files and programs. However, groups are not hierarchical; in other words you cannot have a group within a group.

Groups can be shown in two ways, as group icons, in which case their contents are hidden, or as visible groups, in which case the icons within the group are also visible. Groups can be switched between being visible and "iconised" using the mouse.

Menus

Menus provide general purpose commands and features that allow you to perform tasks that are not provided in the form of icons. Activating a menu produces a drop-down list of options from which a choice may be made.

Using the Mouse

As noted, the mouse is used extensively for selecting and issuing commands within Windows and so it is important to be aware of what is possible. The main mouse operations are discussed below.

Moving

The mouse position is represented on screen as a mouse cursor, usually a pointing arrow but occasionally it may be shown as some other shape such as a cross, double headed arrow, hand etc. Different shapes are used to denote different functions and behaviour.

The mouse cursor moves in synchronisation with the mouse itself. For example, moving the mouse away from you should move the cursor up the screen, whilst moving the mouse towards you moves the cursor down the screen. Similarly moving the mouse left and right moves the cursor accordingly.

As you move the mouse you may notice the cursor change shape occasionally, especially when it is positioned over the border (edge) of a group. These different shapes signify that the mouse could be used to manipulate the group if required. We will come back to this later.

Clicking

In addition to moving the mouse cursor, the mouse can be used to activate icons, groups and menu options when the cursor is positioned over them by pressing its buttons. Clicking is the process of pressing and releasing the mouse button just once, and is used to select menu choices.

By default, Windows assumes that the left mouse button will be used for this purpose. If necessary this can be changed so that the right mouse button is used instead. This is covered in the reference manuals supplied with the Windows software.

Double-clicking

Double-clicking is achieved by pressing and releasing the mouse button twice in quick succession. This is used to activate icons and groups. As with single-clicking, Windows assumes that the left mouse button will be used.

A tip worth noting is that you need to keep the mouse perfectly still when double clicking. If it is moved, Windows sees the two button presses as two separate clicks rather than one double-click. Not surprisingly some newcomers to Windows find double-clicking somewhat awkward, although with a little practice it will soon become second nature.

Right-clicking

Some programs, such as Word, support the use of the right mouse button as a shortcut to some common operations. This is pressed and released in the same way as the left mouse button.

Dragging

Some tasks require that you move or copy information with the mouse, and this is accomplished by dragging. This means that you position the mouse cursor on the item that you want to move, press and hold the left mouse button, then drag the cursor to the required destination. Only then do you release the mouse button.

Other Mouse Operations

Occasionally it may be necessary to use the mouse in some other way. For example, Word allows a paragraph of text to be selected by *triple-clicking* the left mouse button. This is obviously more difficult still than a double click, so it may be easier to use the keyboard shortcut than to rely on the mouse.

Using the Keyboard

In addition to using the mouse to issue commands, Windows allows the keyboard to be used to perform the same tasks. There are in fact two ways of using the keyboard – *hot keys* and *shortcuts*.

* A hot key is a key or combination of keys that can be pressed to simulate mouse actions.

* A shortcut is a key combination, often involving the CTRL, ALT or SHIFT keys, that duplicates the effects of several mouse operations.

Shortcut keystroke combinations often save time as they minimise the number of keystrokes or mouse clicks that are required to perform a task or series of tasks.

Identifying Hot Keys

Hot keys are recognisable on screen as they have an underline beneath the letter or character to be used. For example, the first menu option in most applications is File, with the underline signifying that F is the hot key for this option.

To use a hot key, the ALT key is pressed and held whilst the hot key character is pressed and released. This will trigger the appropriate action, as if you had clicked on the item with the mouse. However, if you want to select an option from a menu that is currently displayed, the hot key alone may be pressed.

Identifying Shortcuts

Shortcut keystrokes can be identified when a menu has been dropped-down, as they are shown alongside the appropriate menu options.

To use a shortcut key combination, press the indicated keys, remembering the CTRL, ALT and SHIFT will all have to be held down whilst other keys are pressed.

Figure 1.3 shows the File menu options available from the Windows Program Manager, together with their hotkeys and shortcuts.

Figure 1-3.
File menu
options.

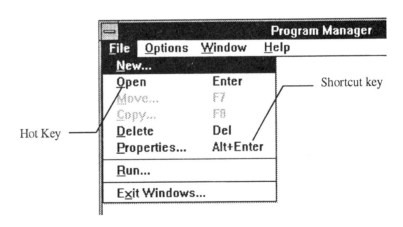

As you can see, each of the hot keys is underlined whilst the shortcut key combinations are shown to the right of the options.

Windows Applications

The different techniques that can be used may appear somewhat daunting to the novice Windows user, but this need not be so. Windows is designed to be intuitive; in other words you should be able to work out what you need to do to achieve a certain goal just by looking at the screen.

In fact a good way to learn to use Windows is to do just that – start an application (the Solitaire game is a good one to try) and use the mouse to see what happens if you click, double-click and drag. Solitaire is very similar to the card game commonly known as *patience*, and supports all of the mouse and keyboard options when you are playing the game.

However, before proceeding there are just a few fundamental operations that you need to be aware of.

Running an Application

An application can be run by double-clicking its icon. Alternatively if you can't successfully double-click yet, then single click the icon to highlight it and press the ENTER key – this is the shortcut key.

If you can't find the icon for the program you want to run, but you know the location and name of the program, then you can use the Run command under the File menu. If you choose File, Run a dialogue box similar to Figure 1.4 will be displayed, allowing you to type in the location and name of the program you want to run.

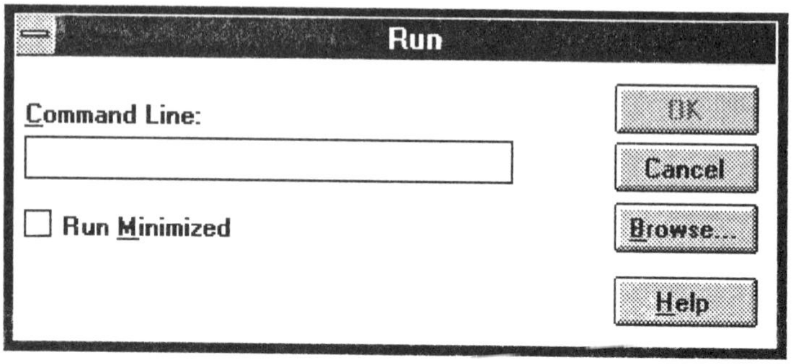

*Figure 1.4.
The Run
dialogue box.*

```
┌────────────────────────────────────────────────────────┐
│ ═                         Run                           │
├────────────────────────────────────────────────────────┤
│                                                         │
│  Command Line:                            ┌──────────┐  │
│                                           │    OK    │  │
│  ┌────────────────────────────────────┐  └──────────┘  │
│  │                                    │  ┌──────────┐  │
│  └────────────────────────────────────┘  │  Cancel  │  │
│                                           └──────────┘  │
│  ☐ Run Minimized                          ┌──────────┐  │
│                                           │ Browse...│  │
│                                           └──────────┘  │
│                                           ┌──────────┐  │
│                                           │   Help   │  │
│                                           └──────────┘  │
└────────────────────────────────────────────────────────┘
```

Into the *Command Line* box you would type the drive, directory and filename of the program you want to run. For example the DOS Editor can be run by entering

C:\DOS\EDIT.COM

Closing an Application

When you have finished with an application you should close it down. Normally there will be an Exit option on the File menu that will allow you to do this, but you can also use the standard shortcut – ALT+F4.

You can also use a special feature of the program's window, known as the control button. This is situated at the very top left of the window, as shown in Figure 1.5.

Single-clicking the control button produces a special menu, known as the control menu. One of the options on the control menu is Close, which will shut down the current application. In fact double-clicking the control menu also has the same effect.

Figure 1.5. The Control button.

Control Button

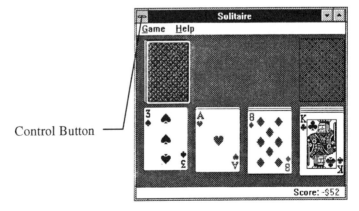

Minimising, Maximising and Restoring

When a program is running, its on-screen window can be shown in one of three different states; *Minimised*, *Maximised* or *Restored*.

- A minimised window is shown as an icon at the bottom left of the desktop area.

- A maximised window will completely fill the desktop area.

- A restored window is in a flexible condition, being neither maximised nor minimised. Instead, the position and size of the window can be adjusted using the mouse

The controls that are used to minimise and maximise a window are shown in Figure 1.6.

Figure 1.6. Minimise and Maximise buttons.

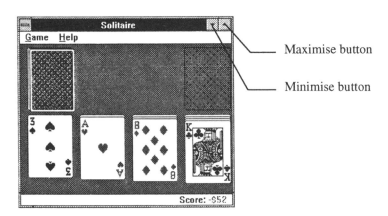

Maximise button

Minimise button

There are no corresponding controls for resizing or repositioning a restored Window, although there are *Size* and *Move* options available through the control menu. Instead, all that is necessary to resize the window is to position the cursor over its edge and click and drag that edge to its new position. If you want to reposition the whole window then move the cursor onto the title bar and click and drag to move it.

As you move or resize the window you will see a transparent grey outline whilst you are dragging; the content of the window will be redrawn when you release the mouse button.

Having maximised a window, the maximise button will change to show a double-headed arrow. This is the restore button and will appear as shown in Figure 1.7.

Figure 1.7. The Restore button.

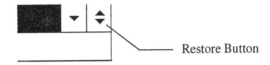

Restore Button

If the desktop is completely filled by a maximised application then all other windows will be hidden. If you wanted to access one of these hidden applications then you would need to use one of the following techniques.

The Task List

Once you have several applications running it may become confusing as to exactly what has been closed and what has not. The task list will show you exactly what is currently active, and will allow you to control each of the applications.

The task list is displayed when you press ALT+ESC, or when you choose the Switch To option from a control menu. The task list appears as shown in Figure 1.8.

Figure 1.8. The Task List.

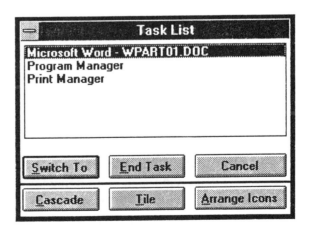

Three programs are listed in this example, Microsoft Word, Program Manager (the one that contains your icons) and Print Manager. The one at the top of the list, Word, is the one that we are currently working with.

The buttons beneath the list allow you to manage the programs as follows:

- **Switch To** will activate the highlighted program, and remove the task list from the screen. Note that activating (which takes you into an existing program), is not the same as running (which executes another copy of that program).

- **End Task** is the same as closing the application from the control menu or with a File, Exit command.

- **Cancel** causes the task list to be removed from the screen, without taking any other action at all.

- **Cascade** and **Tile** cause Windows to position each of the programs so that some or all of each of their windows is visible.

- **Arrange Icons** moves all of the minimised programs to the bottom of the screen, positioning their icons at equal intervals.

Switching Between Applications

In addition to using the task list to switch between applications, you can also use some keyboard shortcuts.

- ALT+TAB causes a box to be displayed in the centre of the screen containing the name of a program. If you continue to hold the ALT key down and repeatedly press the TAB key, Windows will cycle through each of the active applications. When you release the TAB key you will activate the program whose name is displayed.

- ALT+ESC also cycles through the applications, although rather than just displaying each one's name it will redraw the whole of its display, which makes it slower. However, you may find this a clearer way of switching between programs.

For example, assuming you are currently working with Word, and you also have Paintbrush and Program Manager running, pressing ALT+TAB will display the name of the previous application you used, Paintbrush:

 Paintbrush - (Untitled)

Holding the ALT key down and pressing TAB again displays the name of the next program in the sequence, in this case Program Manager:

 Program Manager

If TAB is pressed a third time with the ALT key held down, then the box will show the details for Word:

 Microsoft Word - Document3

Remember that to obtain this sequence the ALT key must be held down continually, only being released when the box shows the name of the program you want to switch to.

In addition to using the keyboard, the mouse can also be used to activate an application providing you can see any part of its window on screen. Simply clicking on something that is in the background will bring it forwards and make it completely visible.

Closing Windows

When you have finished working with your applications, it is very important to shut Windows down before you switch the PC off. Failure to observe this simple precaution could lead to serious problems later on.

The way to shut Windows down is to switch to the Program Manager using any of the previous techniques, and choose File, Exit or choose the Close option from its control menu. You will be prompted to confirm that you wish to exit Windows with the dialogue box shown in Figure 1.9.

Figure 1.9.
Exiting Windows.

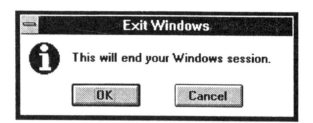

On clicking the OK button, or pressingENTER, you will be returned to the DOS prompt. Only at this stage should you switch the PC off.

Installing Word

Before you can go ahead and use Word, you need to ensure that it is installed onto your computer. It may be that the software was pre-installed onto your system, which means that it should be ready to run and you can skip onto Chapter Two to learn how to use it.

However, if this is not the case (if you bought the program yourself, for example), then you need to follow the remainder of this chapter in order to get the software onto the PC.

Backing up the Disks

The first stage of installation is to make a security backup of the original disks. You need to do this just in case something happens to the disks now or in the future.

The easiest way to make a backup of the disks is to use the DOS DISKCOPY command as follows:

- Make sure that you have as many blank, formatted disks as you have original disks. Usually there are 9 or more separate disks, depending on whether you have 3½" or 5¼" disks. Your blank disks must be the same size and capacity as the originals.

- Make sure that your original disks are write protected. See your DOS and PC manuals for further information.

- Ensure that your computer is ready for you to issue commands, i.e. it is at the DOS prompt.

- Place the first of the original disks in the drive.

- If you have two identical floppy disk drives, place the first blank disk into the second drive.

- Issue the DISKCOPY command

  DISKCOPY A: A: or DISKCOPY B: B: if using a single drive

  DISKCOPY A: B: if using two drives (NOTE: Drive A must hold the original and Drive B must hold the blank disk)

- Follow any on-screen prompts, changing disks when necessary with a single-drive system.

- When the process has finished you will be asked if you want to copy another disk. Respond by typing Y, then repeat the above steps for the remaining disks.

- Remember to label each of the disks as they are copied so that you can identify them when they are used to install the software.

Having made your backups they should now be used for the remainder of the installation process, and your original disks stored somewhere safe.

The Installation Process

Your are now ready to install the software, so take the first of your backed-up disks and place it into the floppy drive. Start Windows, then choose the File, Run command from Program Manager.

When prompted for the command line, type in A:\SETUP if using drive A for the floppies, or B:\SETUP if using drive B. This tells Windows to run the setup program on the floppy disk. If it reports an error then make sure that you have the correct disk inserted into the drive and that the drive door is correctly closed.

As setup runs it prompts you for information. For example, the first time it is used it will ask for your name and company name so that the software can be registered to you. It will also ask you to specify what type of installation you want – Typical, Custom/Complete or Laptop.

"Typical" is likely to be the most appropriate as it ensures that all key features are installed for you. However, if you have plenty of free disk space, the "Complete/Custom" option is best as it guarantees that every feature is installed for you. The "Laptop" installation is useful only if you have limited free disk space, as it requires the smallest amount of the three techniques.

As you proceed through the Setup program you will be prompted to change disks, and may be asked for further information. If you are unsure of exactly what is required then consult the Word documentation.

Having been successfully installed, Word will require you to restart Windows, and may need you to reboot the PC. It will tell you on-screen exactly what you must do, and it is important to follow the instructions provided.

The Word Group

Once installed onto your PC, the Word icons are placed into a separate group within Program Manager. The icons within the group are shown in Figure 1.10.

Figure 1.10.
The Word group.

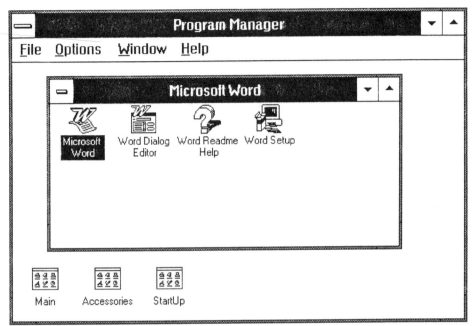

These icons are used to run Word and its associated utilities. The leftmost one, with the title Microsoft Word, runs the Word program itself, whilst the second one launches a utility called the dialogue editor, for use in conjunction with macros. The question-mark icon will display the "readme" file which contains addenda and updates to the printed documentation, plus any late-breaking news about the Word software. The final icon, Word Setup allows you to reconfigure the software at a later date.

Summary

Word is one of the most flexible and powerful Word processors available for the Windows environment. It has a proven track record, and is part of a complete range of applications that cater for all business needs.

All Word commands can be selected using the mouse, keyboard, or a combination of both. This makes it easy for novices and experienced users alike.

Similarly the process of installing Word onto the PC is very straightforward and should present no problems.

Self Test

1   What is the name of the suite of programs that includes Microsoft Word, Excel and Powerpoint?

2   How does version 6 of Word for Windows differ from version 6 of Word for the Macintosh?

3   What does Intellisense do?

4   How much memory is needed in the PC to run Word, and how much more is recommended?

5   Which versions of DOS and Windows are required to run Word?

6   What is the maximum length of a DOS filename?

7   Which of the following filenames are valid?
        REPORT.DOC
        NEW DATA.DOC
        INFORMATION

8   How do you start Windows?

9   What is an icon?

10   How do you run an application from within Windows?

TWO
Starting Off

Key Learning Points In This Chapter

- Loading Word for Windows
- Understanding the Word workplace
- Toolbars
- Rulers
- Display options

Loading Word for Windows

If you have just installed Word by following the instructions in Chapter One you will have been asked to rerun Windows at the end of the Setup procedure.

If Word is already on your computer and you are beginning to use the book from this point you must start-up Windows and look for the Word icon. This may be on the opening screen when Windows is loaded as shown in Figure 2.1 or you might have to open a group icon such as Applications or Microsoft Office in order to see the Word icon.

Figure 2.1.
The Windows
desktop.

The Microsoft
Word icon

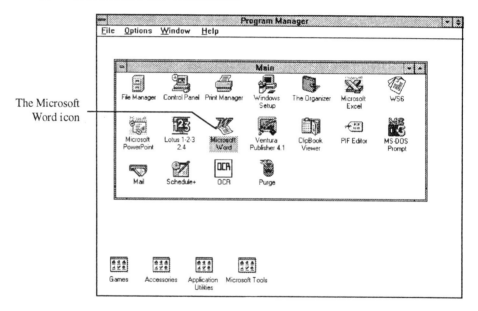

To load Word position the mouse over the Word icon and double click the left mouse button. The length of time Word takes to load will vary from computer to computer, but when loading is complete the screen will appear as shown in Figure 2.2.

Every time Word is loaded a tip of the day is displayed. Click on *OK* to close this dialogue box. If you do not want to display the tip of the day on start-up, clear the check box at the bottom left of the screen.

Figure 2.2.
Tip of the Day.

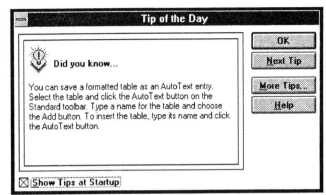

Note: *the book assumes that at this point Word has not been customised in any way. If your system has been installed with customised toolbars your screen may not look the same. It would be preferable to re-install Word without customisation for the purposes of working with this book.*

The Main Word Window

When Word is loaded a new, blank document is displayed as shown in Figure 2.3.

Figure 2.3.
The Word screen.

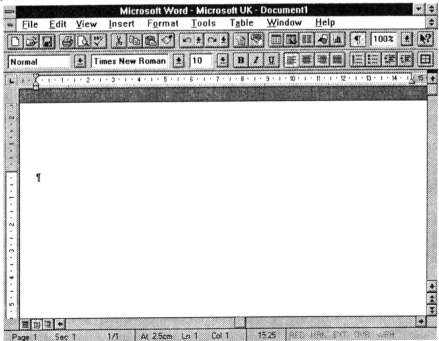

Toolbars

As in all Windows applications the toolbars allow quick access to commonly used commands. On starting Word the Standard and Formatting toolbars are displayed.

1   Move the pointer over one of the toolbar buttons and notice the name is displayed in a small box below the selected button. This is called a *ToolTip*. A brief description of what the button does is displayed at the bottom of the screen.

2   Position the pointer anywhere on the toolbar and press the right mouse button. This lists all the available toolbars with a tick alongside those that are currently displayed.

3   Click on the *Formatting* option to clear the tick and the Formatting toolbar is no longer displayed.

4   Press the right mouse button and click on the *Formatting* option again to redisplay the toolbar.

Selecting Toolbars from this menu displays the toolbar dialogue box. This provides options to enlarge toolbar buttons, to add colour to buttons and to hide the ToolTips. New toolbars can be created and buttons added or removed from existing toolbars. See Chapter Twelve for more information on these options.

Exercise

1   Display all the available toolbars and then hide all but the Standard and Formatting ones.

The default position for the Standard and Formatting toolbars is immediately below the menu bar. As you will have seen when performing the exercise, with the exception of the Drawing toolbar which is positioned at the bottom of the screen, other toolbars are stacked below the Formatting. By default the toolbars are *anchored* in these positions. Any toolbar can be *floated* in order that it can be moved around the screen to the required position.

To float an anchored toolbar, position the pointer on a blank part of the toolbar, hold down the SHIFT key and double-click. The toolbar can now be moved around the screen by dragging the title bar. It can be resized by dragging the edge or corner. To anchor a floating toolbar, double-click the toolbar title bar.

Exercise

1	Display the Drawing toolbar.
2	Make it a floating toolbar and resize it to be positioned horizontally at the top of the page, immediately below the Formatting toolbar.
3	Re-anchor the toolbar.
4	Hide the toolbar.

Rulers

If there is no ruler currently being displayed on your screen it can be selected from the View menu. The vertical ruler will only be displayed in page layout view or print preview. The ruler is used for setting page and column widths, tab stops and indents which are described in Chapter Four, as well as table and column widths which are described in Chapter Nine.

Status Bar

At the bottom of the screen are the horizontal scroll bar and the status bar which displays information about the current document or the task you are working on. The exact information displayed will vary according to what you are doing.

On the left of the horizontal scroll bar there are three buttons which allow you to change between Normal, Page Layout and Outline view. Positioning the pointer over a button will display a brief description of that button.

When typing into a document the status bar gives information about the text on the screen. Figure 2.4 is an example of such a status bar.

Figure 2.4.
The Status bar.

Page 4 refers to the printed page number which can be customised to display any specified number. *Sec 1* is the section number. A document can be broken into a number of sections (see Chapter Nine). *4/5* is the actual page reference. In this case the cursor is currently on page four of a five page document. The next section of the status bar gives the exact position of the cursor in terms of centimetres, line number and column number. (The unit of measure can be changed from centimetres to other units such as inches or points). The next section displays the time which is continually updated. The last five sections of the status bar in Figure 2.4 are mode indicators which can be switched on or off by double-clicking on them. For example, double-clicking on *OVR* turns overtype on; double-clicking on it again turns overtype off. These modes will be explained in later chapters but the abbreviations are as follows:-

REC	Record macro
MRK	Use revision marks
EXT	Select text in extend mode
OVR	Toggle between overtype and insert
WPH	Help for WordPerfect users

Displaying a Document

There are a number of options available for displaying a document which may be seen from the View menu shown in Figure 2.5.

Normal View

The default mode is normal view. This is a simplified view of the document which preferable when writing and editing text. In this view mode the page layout is not shown in terms of margins etc., but a dotted line indicates page breaks.

Figure 2.5.
The View menu.

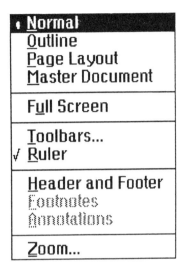

To switch between Normal, Page Layout and Outline the appropriate selection may be made from the View menu or the buttons on the horizontal scroll bar may be used. The left most button represents Normal view followed by Page Layout and Outline.

Page Layout View

Page Layout is WYSIWYG (What You See Is What You Get). This means that the document is displayed with all tables, columns, pictures, graphics and images fully formatted in the position they will be printed in. Furthermore the vertical ruler is displayed showing where the top and bottom margins are located. Headers and footers are also shown in a lighter shade.

Figure 2.6 is an example of a screen displaying in Page Layout view.

Outline View

In this mode a document can be reduced to only the main headings which makes scrolling through a lengthy document much quicker and the hierarchy of topics can easily be changed.

Figure 2.6.
Page Layout
view.

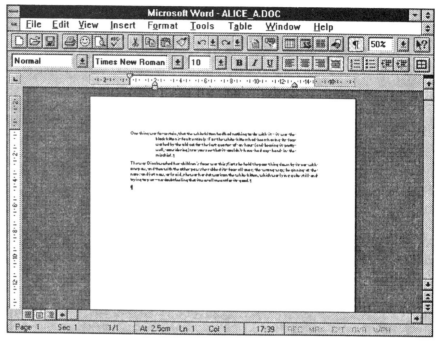

Full Screen

Although it is useful to have access to toolbars and to be able to view rulers and scrollbars, these features inevitably reduce the amount of screen space left for the document. Selecting *View | Full Screen* removes all the screen elements, replacing this space with the document. One small icon is displayed at the bottom right of the screen which, by clicking on it once, returns all the screen elements.

When in Full Screen mode menus can be accessed using the keyboard shortcuts. For example, to access the File menu, press ALT+F and then a required selection may be made in the usual way. Using the keyboard shortcuts certain elements of the screen display can be invoked. For example the following displays the vertical scrollbar:-

1   ALT+T   Displays the toolbar menu

2   O   Selects Options

3 Select the *View* tab

4 Check the *Vertical Scroll Bar* box

5 Click on the *OK* button

Exercise

1 Set the display to full screen and then add the Status Bar. Return to normal display.

Print Preview

Print Preview enables full pages to be viewed at a reduced size in order that the document's layout can be adjusted before printing. Print Preview is accessed either through the File menu or by pressing the Print Preview button on the Standard Toolbar . The options available within Print Preview are discussed in Chapter Four.

Summary

The Word screen offers a comprehensive set of basic features that you will find useful during document creation and editing. These will be used extensively in later chapters in the book. Furthermore, many of these features can be customised or changed to better reflect the specific type of work you are doing and some examples of this can be seen in Chapter Five.

Self Test

1 With Windows running, what is required to load Word for Windows?

2 Which toolbars are displayed by default when Word is started?

3 Describe two ways of displaying the Borders toolbar.

4 What is required to make the Borders toolbar "float"?

5 What is required to re-anchor the Borders toolbar?

6   Describe two ways of hiding the Borders toolbar.

7   What is required to show the vertical ruler?

8   What is the difference between Page 7 and 7/7 on the status bar?

9   What is required to turn overtype on?

10   What is the effect of selecting *View | Full Screen*.

THREE
Creating a Document

Key Learning Points In This Chapter

- Type text into a document
- Name and save document onto the disk
- Close and Open documents
- Copy, delete and move text
- Using AutoCorrect and AutoText

Introduction

On starting Word a new empty document is automatically opened. By default it is assumed that you are using 8.5 by 11 inch paper with 1.25 inch left and right margins, and 1 inch top and bottom margins. The vertical bar or *insertion point* is flashing at the top left hand corner of the screen and when you type text the characters appear on the screen or *document window*.

Typing Text

Type in the following passage. Do not worry if you make some mistakes as these can be corrected later. However, if you mistype a character then the BACKSPACE key [⇐] may be pressed to delete the last character/s typed. You do not have to press ENTER at the end of each line as Word will do this for you automatically. When you reach the end of the first paragraph you must press the ENTER key twice before continuing with the second paragraph.

> **One thing was certain, that the white kitten had had nothing to do with it - it was the black kitten's fault entirely. For the white kitten had been having its face washed by the old cat for the last quarter of an hour (and bearing it pretty well, considering): so you see that it couldn't have had any hand in the mischief.**

> **The way Dinah washed her children's faces was this: first she held the poor thing down by its ear with one paw, and then with the other paw she rubbed its face all over, the wrong way, beginning at the nose: and just now, as I said, she was hard at work on the white kitten, which was lying quite still and trying to purr - no doubt feeling that it was all meant for its good.**

Saving Text

As with any work on a computer it is important to regularly save because at this stage your text is only being stored in the computer's memory, as opposed to the disk, and if the power were to fail it would be lost.

There are two ways to access the Save As dialogue box, either by selecting *File | Save* or by clicking on the *Save* button, ▣ on the Standard toolbar. Figure 3.1 shows the Save As dialogue box. The default filename supplied by Word of DOC1.DOC may be displayed in the *File Name* box and this may be overwritten with your own filename.

Figure 3.1.
The Save As
dialogue box.

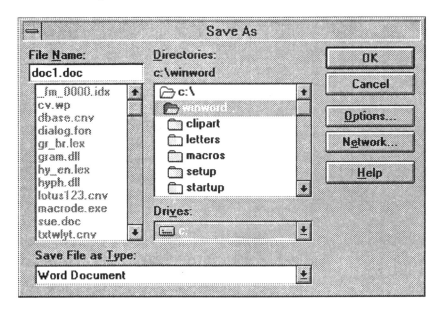

On starting Word the default drive is the drive Word was installed on. This will usually be drive C on a standalone PC, but if you are working on a network it may be a different drive letter. The default directory is Winword which is shown under the *Directories* part of the dialogue box. On page 26 of Chapter One you were shown how to create a directory on your hard disk called STEPWORD into which your work will be saved.

1 Double click on C:\ in the *Directories* list to return to the root directory.

2 Use the scroll bar to display STEPWORD.

3 Position the mouse pointer over it and double click. Figure 3.2 shows how the dialogue box now appears.

Figure 3.2.
Save As dialogue
box showing
required
directory.

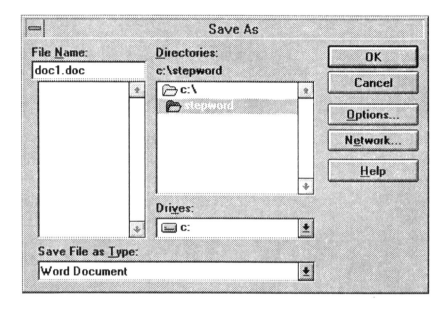

There are no files in this directory yet, but as you create the example files used in this book they will be stored in this directory.

4 With the insertion point flashing in the *File Name* box, type **ALICE_1** and either press ENTER or click once on *OK*.

5 Unless it has been disabled, you will now see the Summary Info dialogue box, as shown in Figure 3.3.

Figure 3.3.
Summary Info
dialogue box

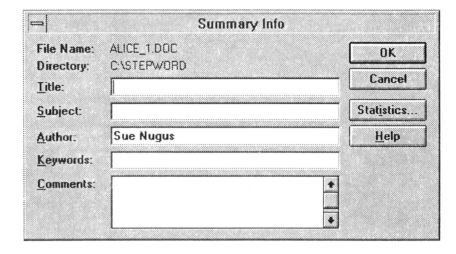

The Summary Info dialogue box allows you to enter summary information about the document you are saving. You do not have to fill out all the information, but the *Title* and *Keywords* are particularly useful because if you cannot remember the name of the file containing particular information, you can use the ***Edit | Find*** command to search for a document title or for keywords in a document. This will then tell you the name of the file containing the information.

6　Click in the *Title* box and type **Alice Through The Looking Glass**

7　Click in the *Keywords* box and type **Alice, kitten, Dinah**

8　Click *OK* to complete the save operation.

Note: *If you do not want to use the Summary Info or it is not displayed on your system you can turn it on or off through **Tools | Options** and select the Save tab.*

A Note On Saving

Word has a number of special features available when saving files, two of which are important to be aware of at this stage.

There is a *fast save* option which means that when a file is saved after changes or updates have been made, only those parts of the document that need to be changed are saved instead of the whole document. This can make a considerable difference to the length of time it takes to save large files and files containing pictures and images. However, if a problem should occur with the system whilst working on a document it is more likely that the file may become corrupted.

There is also an *automatic save* option which will save your document every so many minutes - the number is decided by you. If you know that you are not very good at remembering to save regularly it is worth considering the use of this feature. However, remember that if you are editing a document and you want to return to the previous version you might not be able to do so if it has automatically been saved in the meantime.

To set or reset the fast save and automatic save features select *Tools | Options* and click on the *Save* tab. Figure 3.4 shows this screen.

Figure 3.4.
The Save
Options dialogue
box.

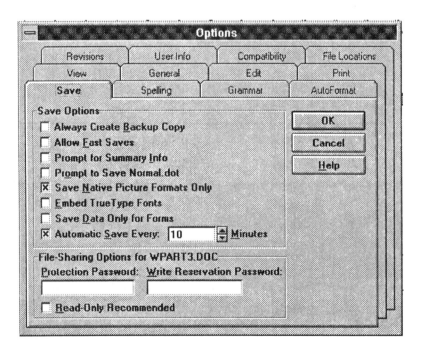

Closing a Document

When a document is saved it remains on the screen and is available for further use. If the document is no longer required it may be closed by selecting the *File | Close*. Incidentally, if the document had not been saved when *Close* is selected a warning is displayed on the screen which allows you to cancel the *Close* operation in order to first save the document.

1　Close the ALICE_1 document by selecting *File | Close*.

Opening a Document

There are three ways to retrieve, or *open* a document from disk.

Selecting *File | Open* or clicking on the *Open* button　displays the Open dialogue box shown in Figure 3.5.

Figure 3.5. Open dialogue box.

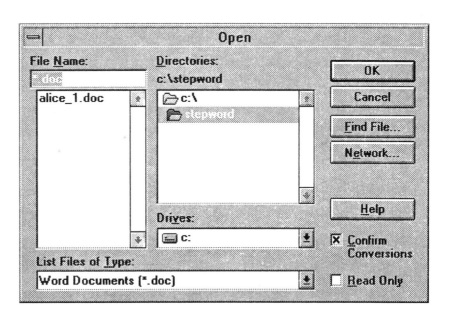

The dialogue box will be displaying the .DOC files in the current directory. As ALICE_1 was saved in the STEPWORD directory this will automatically be displayed. If the incorrect directory is shown the correct one must be accessed by double clicking on C:\ and then scrolling through the list of directories until the required one is displayed. Double clicking on the required directory will make it active and will display the .DOC files.

1   Double click on ALICE_1.

2   The document is opened with the insertion point positioned at the beginning.

Another way to open a document that you have recently been working on is by selecting it from the bottom of the File menu. Figure 3.6 is an example of the File menu.

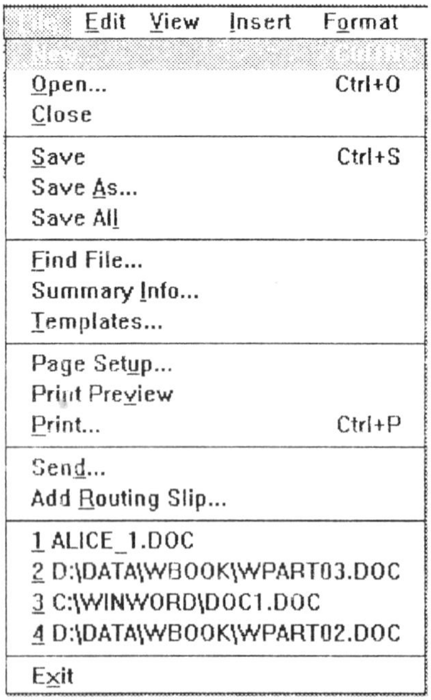

Figure 3.6.
The File menu.

```
        Edit   View   Insert   Format
    ─────────────────────────────────────

    Open...                      Ctrl+O
    Close
    ─────────────────────────────────────
    Save                         Ctrl+S
    Save As...
    Save All
    ─────────────────────────────────────
    Find File...
    Summary Info...
    Templates...
    ─────────────────────────────────────
    Page Setup...
    Print Preview
    Print...                     Ctrl+P
    ─────────────────────────────────────
    Send...
    Add Routing Slip...
    ─────────────────────────────────────
    1 ALICE_1.DOC
    2 D:\DATA\WBOOK\WPART03.DOC
    3 C:\WINWORD\DOC1.DOC
    4 D:\DATA\WBOOK\WPART02.DOC
    ─────────────────────────────────────
    Exit
```

By default the system will list the last four files that were saved. If the files are in a different directory or on a different disk to the current disk and directory their path is also listed. In the above example the current directory is STEPWORD where ALICE_1.DOC is located. To open the file it is only necessary to highlight it on the list and click once with the mouse.

The number of files that may be listed can be changed by selecting *Tools | Options* and clicking on the *General* tab. There is an option on this screen to specify the number of entries in the *Recently Used Files* list. You can choose to display between zero and nine files.

Exercise

1   Using the *Open* button on the Standard toolbar open the ALICE_1 file.

2   With the insertion point at the beginning of the document insert the word ALICE at the beginning of the text.

3   Close the document without saving the change.

4   Open the document again by selecting from the list of files in the File menu.

Editing The Document

Before continuing, read the passage that you have entered and look for any mistakes. Simple typographical errors can be quickly corrected by clicking at the relevant point, which locates the insertion point, and then the appropriate correction may be made. The following keys are useful for this type of editing:-

[⇐] (backspace)   deletes character to left of insertion point.

[DEL]   deletes character to right of insertion point.

[INS]   toggles between insert and overwrite mode (indicated at bottom right of screen).

Having corrected any typographical errors the document should be saved again. Clicking on the *Save* button 🖫 on the Standard toolbar will resave the document using the existing name.

Selecting Text

To do anything with a piece of text it must first be selected. Text can be selected by word, line, sentence, paragraph or document. The following mouse actions are required:

Word   Double click on the word (includes following space).

Line   Click in the selection bar to the left of the line, (inserting 1 line changes mouse pointer arrow when in the selection bar). Drag in the selection bar to select multiple lines.

Sentence   Hold down the CTRL key and click anywhere in the sentence.

Paragraph   Double click in the selection bar or triple click anywhere in the paragraph. Drag in the selection bar to select multiple paragraphs.

Document   Triple click in the selection bar.

Text selection may also be made by positioning the mouse at the beginning of the required text, clicking and dragging to the end. Alternatively the insertion point can be positioned at the beginning of the text to be selected, then holding the SHIFT key, click at the end of the required range.

Exercise

> **1**   Select the following from the ALICE_1 file using the most efficient method.
>
> **2**   The second line.
>
> **3**   The text "(and bearing it pretty well, considering)"
>
> **4**   The first paragraph.

Exercise Cont.

---

5 The word "Dinah".

6 The text "and then with the other paw she rubbed its face all over, the wrong way, beginning at the nose: and just now".

7 The sentence "One thing was certain, that the white kitten had had nothing to do with it -it was the black kitten's fault entirely."

8 The whole document.

Tip: *If you did not select the text that you wanted, click outside the selection and then try again.*

The DEL and BACKSPACE keys are fine for deleting the odd character, but are not an efficient way of deleting larger amounts of text.

Deleting Using Select and Cut

To delete the word "old" in the first paragraph,

1 Position the pointer somewhere in the word and double click.

The word is selected which is shown by it being highlighted. Notice that the space following the word is automatically included in the selection.

2 Click on the *Cut* button on the Standard toolbar and the selected text is deleted from the document.

3 To replace the text click on the *Undo* button.

4 And, if you change your mind again and want to remove the word after all, click the *Redo* button.

Simply clicking on the *Undo* and *Redo* buttons automatically refers to the last action taken, but by clicking on the arrow to the right of the button allows you to scroll through a series of previous actions in order to return a document to the way it was before a number of changes were made.

Note: *Because a number of changes in a series can depend on preceding changes, all the actions that precede the selected one will be undone.*

When text is cut it is placed on the *Clipboard* and may be copied into a new location in the same document, to another Word document, or to another Windows application. It is also possible to delete text by selecting the appropriate range and pressing the DEL key. However, it is not possible to use this text elsewhere as it has been removed rather than placed on the clipboard. The only way text deleted in this way may be recovered is by selecting *Undo*.

Replacing Text

If a selected piece of text is to be deleted and different text put in its place the easiest way to do this is to select the required text for deletion and then, ensuring the system is in insert mode, type the new text. It is not necessary to first cut or delete the selected text as it will automatically be removed when you start entering new text.

Moving Text

There are two ways in which text can be moved. The first is to use the *cut* and *paste* options and the second is to use the *drag* and *drop* facility.

To illustrate these two methods of moving, the first sentence of the Alice extract will be moved to the beginning of the second paragraph.

1 Select the sentence by positioning the pointer on the sentence and CTRL click.

2 Use the *Cut* button to place the text on the clipboard.

3 Move the pointer to the beginning of the second paragraph and click to position the insertion point there.

4   Click on the *Paste* button ▦ to display the text at the new location.

Tip: *If the same text is required at another location, for example at the end of the second paragraph, position the insertion point and click on the Paste button again. The text that was cut remains on the clipboard until something else is cut or copied onto it.*

To perform the above move using the drag and drop facility, first click the Undo button to return the sentence to the beginning of the document.

1   Select the sentence with CTRL+CLICK.

2   Position the mouse pointer on the selection and it will change to a left-pointing arrow.

3   Hold down the left mouse button which will produce a small, feint dotted box and a dotted insertion point.

4   While still holding down the left mouse button, drag the dotted insertion point to the beginning of the second paragraph and then release the mouse button.

5   Click away from the selected text to remove the highlighting.

Copying Text

Copying text is very similar to moving text and may also be performed using the two steps of copying and pasting, or by dragging and dropping.

To copy the sentence "The way Dinah washed her children's faces was this:" in ALICE_1 to the end of the document using the copy and paste option:

1   Select the text by double clicking on the sentence.

2   Click on the *Copy* button ▦.

3   Move the insertion point to the end of the document (press a space if necessary after the full stop).

4   Click on the *Paste* button .

To perform the same copy using the drag and drop facility, first select the text as before.

1   Hold the CTRL key, point to the selected text and hold down the left mouse button

2   Move the dotted insertion point to the required location

3   Release the CTRL key and the mouse button and the copy is performed.

Exercise

1   Using the move and delete facilities, reset the Alice extract as it was originally.

2   Copy the first paragraph at the end of the document.

You may or may not have to enter or remove spaces when using the drag and drop feature. This depends on whether the *smart-cut-and-paste* feature is active on your system. To enable the feature:

1   Select *Tools |Options.*

2   Click on the *Edit* tab and check the *Use Smart-Cut and Paste* box.

Word will now insert or delete spaces automatically when selections of text are moved or copied using drag and drop.

AutoCorrect and AutoText

The AutoCorrect feature in Word can be used in two ways. In the first instance you can store words that you commonly misspell so that when you type the misspelled word AutoCorrect will replace it with the correct spelling, while you are typing. Word supplies some common mistakes and you can add your own to the list. In addition you can use AutoCorrect to fill out long or complicated words so that you enter one or two characters and the system converts this abbreviation to the full word.

AutoCorrect, when activated, works as you type text and does not give you the option to replace a word or an abbreviation. AutoText, on the other hand, allows you to store abbreviations that will be expanded only when you demand them by pressing the F3 function key.

Using AutoCorrect

To see what is currently in the AutoCorrect list select **Tools | AutoCorrect**. Figure 3.7 shows the AutoCorrect dialogue box.

Figure 3.7. AutoCorrect dialogue box.

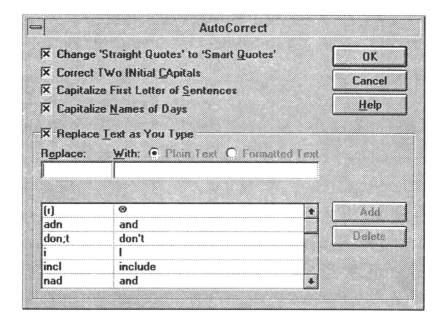

If you, for example, type in 'adn' instead of 'and' AutoCorrect will correct the spelling for you immediately. If you scroll through the list on this dialogue box you can see the other spellings that are provided.

Notice the (r) which will automatically change to the registered trademark symbol, ® . If you wanted to insert this symbol into your text you would simply type (r) and AutoCorrect will convert what you type to ® .

Note: *AutoCorrect only works once the* SPACEBAR *has been pressed.*

In addition to changing specified entries, you can see from Figure 3.7 that you can choose to have AutoCorrect check for capitalisation and quotes.

Note: *Be careful when choosing to have AutoCorrect correct capitalisation if you are working with a technical document which might require unusual use of capital letters.*

To add your own entries to the AutoCorrect list you type the misspelling, or an abbreviation into the *Replace* box and the word you want to use in the *With* box. For example, if you are likely to reference the book title 'Alice In Wonderland' several times in a document you can put an abbreviation, such as 'aiw' into the AutoCorrect list which will automatically be expanded when you type it.

1   Type **aiw** into the *Replace* box.

2   Type **Alice In Wonderland** in the *With* box.

3   Click the *Close* button.

4   In the document type **aiw is a book**.

The abbreviation 'aiw' will automatically be expanded to 'Alice In Wonderland'. If you want to have the book title in italics in your document you can format it in the *With* box and then click on the *Formatted Text* button.

If you do not want to use the AutoCorrect feature you can clear the *Replace Text as you Type* box.

Exercise

1	Add the word 'Alise' to the AutoCorrect list to be replaced with 'Alice'.
2	Add the abbreviation 'lc' to be replaced with 'Lewis Carroll'.
3	Delete the 'aiw' entry made earlier in the chapter.

Using AutoText

AutoText allows you to type an abbreviated piece of text that will be expanded in the same way as AutoCorrect, but only when you press the F3 function key. It is a useful technique to use when you regularly require the same word or string of characters. For example, you might have a product list in which each product number begins with the same characters. You can type the first couple of characters and have AutoText fill out the rest of the reference.

Take the insertion point to the end of the Alice extract and press ENTER a couple of times.

You must type in the full text that is to be entered when the abbreviation is typed.

1   Type: **AW-94001.**

2   Select the text.

3   Select *Edit | AutoText.*

The AutoText dialogue box appears as shown in Figure 3.8.

Figure 3.8.
AutoText
dialogue box.

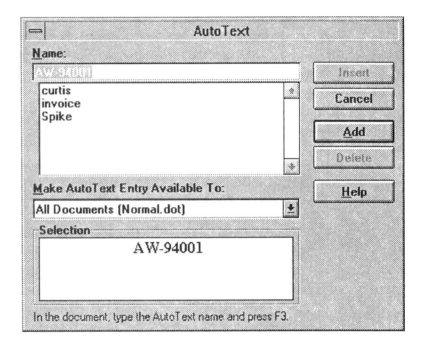

4   In the *Name* box Type: *AW.*

5   Click the *Add* button to return to the document.

To use the AutoText entry:

6   In the document, type *AW* and press F3.

The abbreviation is replaced with 'AW-94001'.

Exercise

1   Close the ALICE_1 document.

2   Open a new document by clicking on the *New* button.

Exercise cont.

> **3**   Enter the following list of products using AutoText to help you.
>
> Microsoft Word
>
> Microsoft Windows
>
> Microsoft PowerPoint
>
> Microsoft Office

Summary

By the end of working through this chapter you will have the mastered the basic skills required to create a document and to perform the fundamental editing that any application requires. Using the AutoText and AutoCorrect features will help you speed up text entry in many cases.

Self Test

1   What does the *insertion point* refer to ?

2   What is the difference between the DEL key and the BACKSPACE keys?

3   Suggest two ways of saving a document for the first time.

4   What is the quickest way to save a document using the same filename after making some changes to it?

5   What problems might the use of the *fast save* cause?

6   How can you change the number of files listed in the File menu?

7   How is a paragraph defined in Word?

8   Suggest two ways of selecting a paragraph of text.

9   Which buttons are used to copy text from one place to another in a
document?

10   How do you add a word to the AutoCorrect list?

FOUR
Formatting Text

Key Learning Points In This Chapter

- Change the appearance of text

- Change the alignment of text

- Paragraph formatting

- Adding borders and shading to paragraphs

Introduction

Word offers a wide range of tools for changing the appearance of a document. For example text can be made bold, put into italics, underlined, to name but a few of the options available. Many of the commonly required formatting options are found on the Formatting toolbar, which is probably already displayed below the Standard toolbar. If this is not case:

1   Select View | Toolbars.

2   Check the Formatting box.

The Formatting toolbar is displayed below the Standard toolbar and is shown in Figure 4.1

Figure 4.1.
Formatting
toolbar.

Changing the Appearance of the Text

As with deleting, moving and copying text it is important to first select the text that is to be formatted before making any changes to its appearance.

1   Select the word "white" in the first paragraph of the Alice extract by positioning the mouse pointer on the word and double clicking.

2   To show this in italic, click on the Italic button **I** on the Formatting toolbar.

3   To make the word both italic and bold, with it still highlighted, click on the Bold button **B**.

4   Finally, to also underline the word, with it still highlighted, click on the Underline button **U**.

Notice that when a formatting option has been applied to some highlighted text the button on the toolbar appears a shade lighter. At this stage, with the word "white" highlighted, the bold, italic and underline buttons are all a lighter shade. If you decided that you did not want the word to be underlined, click again on the underline button. The underlining is removed and the button returns to the darker shade.

Exercise

> **1** Make the word "black" in the first paragraph of the Alice extract bold italic.
>
> **2** Underline the text in parentheses "(and bearing it pretty well, considering)".
>
> **3** Make the word "Dinah" in the second paragraph bold.

Changing the Type Style

Word is capable of producing text in a variety of styles, called fonts and the size of a font can also be adjusted. The size of text is usually measured in points - this book for example has been produced in 12 point Times New Roman. The number of fonts available to you and the range of point sizes is established when Windows is installed. However, certain Windows applications such as Microsoft PowerPoint and CorelDRAW! have options to install additional fonts. Figure 4.2 shows some of the available fonts when the arrow next to the font box is clicked.

Figure 4.2.
Some available fonts.

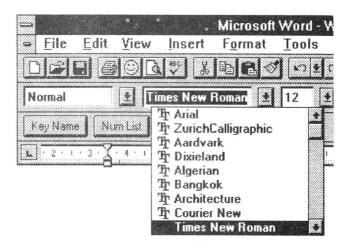

To see the effect of using different fonts and point sizes a heading will be added to the Alice extract which will be displayed in 18 point Arial.

Position the insertion point at the beginning of the text and type the following:

ALICE'S ADVENTURES IN WONDERLAND

LOOKING-GLASS HOUSE

(It is important to press ENTER at the end of each line).

1   Select the two paragraphs by clicking to the left of the first line and dragging the highlighted range over the second line.

2   Click on the arrow to the right of the font box.

3   Click on the required font which in this case is Arial.

4   The selected text has changed in style, but is still not the right size.

5   Next to the font box is the size box and clicking on the arrow to the right of this box drops down the size options.

6   Click on 18 and the selected text is immediately changed.

The new text should now appear as follows:

ALICE'S ADVENTURES IN WONDERLAND

LOOKING-GLASS HOUSE

Exercise

1   Change the title to Arial, 16 point and make it bold.

2   Use the *Undo* button to return the title to its previous setting.

3   Select the first line of the title and change it to Wingdings.

4   Use the *Undo* button to return the title to its previous setting.

Notice that there are some fonts in the list that display strange characters - Wingdings which was used in the above exercise is one example. The fonts that consist of symbols rather than letters which are available on most installations include Monotype Sorts, MT Extra, Symbol and Wingdings. If you are connected to a Postscript printer you will probably also have Zapf Dingbats.

Note: *A point is the standard measurement for text used by the publishing industry. 72 points equals one inch, 36 points is half an inch and so on. Text for business letters, reports etc., will normally be in either 10 or 12 point.*

Changing the Alignment

The title that has now been inserted into the Alice extract would look better centred rather than left aligned which it is now.

To the right of the *Underline* button on the Formatting toolbar there are four alignment buttons; *Align Left*, *Centre*, *Align Right* and *justify* respectively.

To centre the title:

1 Select both lines and click on the *Centre* button 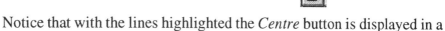.

Notice that with the lines highlighted the *Centre* button is displayed in a lighter shade.

The *Justify* button lays the text out across a line in order that the left and right margins are aligned.

2 Select the first paragraph and click on the justify button .

Repeating Formats with the Format Painter

Having formatted a section of text using the options on the standard and formatting toolbars the *Format Painter* button on the Standard toolbar allows existing formatting to be applied to another selection of text.

1   Select the text "**it was the black kitten's fault entirely.**" and make it bold using the *Bold* button.

2   With the text still highlighted click on the *Format Painter* button 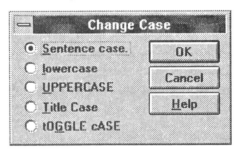. When the mouse pointer is moved there is a paintbrush to the left of it.

3   Now highlight the text "**she was hard at work on the white kitten,**" and when the mouse button is released the bold formatting is automatically copied to this highlighted section of text

If another section of text is also to be bold, click again on the *Format Painter* button and then highlight the text to be formatted.

Changing the Case

Word allows for the case of text to be changed without having to retype the text. This is done by selecting the *Format | Change Case.* The *Change Case* dialogue box may be seen in Figure 4.3.

Figure 4.3. Change Case dialogue box.

The default setting in this dialogue box is *Sentence case* which means that the first character after a full stop will be in upper case and the rest of the words in the sentence will be in lower case. *Lowercase* and *UPPERCASE* change all the characters in the selected range to lower or upper case respectively. *Title Case* displays the first character of each word in upper case and *tOGGLE cASE* displays the selected range in the opposite way to which it is currently showing. This is useful when you have typed in some text without noticing that the CAPS LOCK key was depressed and the following can result:

tHIS SENTENCE WAS TYPED WITH THE cAPS lOCK kEY ON

By selecting the sentence and choosing *tOGGLE cASE* from the Change Case dialogue box it will be displayed as follows:

This sentence was typed with the Caps Lock Key on

Exercise

1   Set the second line of the title in upper and lower case - "**Looking-Glass House**".

2   Capitalise the word "**Dinah**" in the second paragraph.

Paragraph Formatting

The formatting features covered so far have mainly been concerned with selected pieces of text. In many cases however it is necessary to format whole paragraphs in a document. Although many of the buttons on the Formatting toolbar can be applied to paragraphs, the *Paragraph* option on the Format menu has commands that affect the appearance of the entire selected paragraph, as opposed to selected lines or words.

The definition of a *paragraph* in Word is any amount of text, graphics, objects or other items that are followed by a paragraph mark (¶). A paragraph mark is inserted every time you press ENTER or RETURN. The marks can be hidden or displayed by clicking on the paragraph button on the Standard toolbar.

To apply formats to one or more paragraphs they must first be selected. Any changes made will only affect selected paragraphs. It is not necessary to highlight the whole paragraph as long as the insertion point is in the paragraph to be formatted.

1   Open the ALICE_1 document which you saved in the STEPWORD directory.

2   With the insertion point in the first paragraph, select *Format | Paragraph*.

Figure 4.4 shows the dialogue box that will appear.

Figure 4.4.
Paragraph
dialogue box.

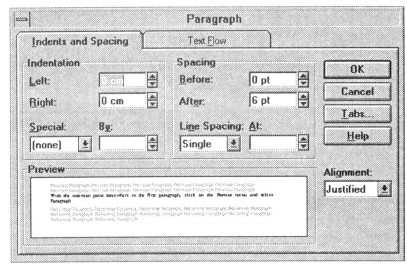

3   To change the spacing of the paragraph click on the arrow to the right of the *Line Spacing* box and select *Double*.

4   Click on *OK* to perform the formatting and return to the document.

Notice that only the first paragraph has been double-spaced. To format the second paragraph, the procedure would have to be repeated with the insertion point somewhere on that paragraph.

If you position the insertion point at the end of the first paragraph and press ENTER, the new paragraph will take the formatting of the previous and will therefore be double-spaced. Type in a couple of lines to see this. All the formatting for a paragraph is stored in the paragraph marker at the end of the paragraph. When moving or copying paragraphs it is important to make sure that the paragraph marker is selected in order that paragraph formatting is retained.

Tip: *Paragraph markers will always be included in a paragraph selection if you click to the left of the paragraph or triple click on the paragraph which ensures the entire paragraph is selected.*

To see the formats of a particular paragraph, click on the *Help* button on the standard toolbar ⟨?⟩ and when the pointer changes to the question mark, click in the paragraph you want to check. Figure 4.5 is an example of the resulting screen. Click the *Help* button again or press ESC to return to the document.

Figure 4.5.
Paragraph
formatting help
screen.

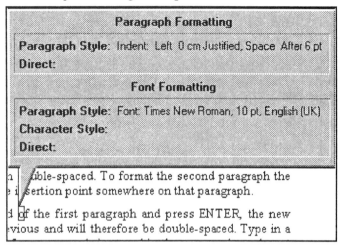

If you want to format a number of paragraphs in the same way, Word provides the facility to create *styles* which can be applied to any number of paragraphs. Creating and applying paragraph styles are explained in Chapter Seven.

Exercise

1   Re-open the ALICE_1 document and using the *Format | Paragraph* commands indent the left and right margins of the first paragraph by .5cm.

2   Set the alignment of the second paragraph to centred.

Setting Indents from the Formatting Toolbar

Two buttons to the right of the Formatting toolbar and allow you to quickly indent the left edge of one or more paragraphs.

Each time you press the *Increase Indent* button the selected paragraph, or one containing the insertion point, is indented by one tab stop. By default Word has preset tab stops every half inch. The *Decrease Indent* button allows you to reverse your action if you indent too far.

Using the Ruler to Set Custom Indents

The ruler at the top of the screen may be used to set custom indents on the left and the right. The symbols on the ruler are markers that control the indents of the current paragraph. The top triangle to the left of the ruler controls the first line of the paragraph and the bottom triangle controls the rest of the paragraph. The small square controls the entire left edge of the paragraph and is called the *paragraph indent marker*. The triangle to the right of the ruler controls the right edge of the paragraph. Figure 4.6 shows these markers.

*Figure 4.6.
Ruler with
paragraph
markers.*

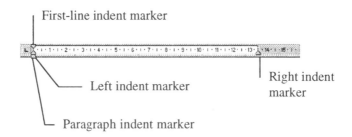

Re-open the ALICE_1 document in order to work with custom indents. In the following exercise the left margin will be indented by 1 inch or 2cms.

1   Place the insertion point somewhere in the first paragraph.

2   Carefully position the mouse pointer on the small square (the paragraph indent marker).

3   Click and drag the marker to the 1 inch or 2cm mark and release the mouse.

Note: *If only the triangle marker moves you did not position the mouse pointer properly on the square. Select **Edit | Undo** and repeat the above procedure.*

To set a right indent the above procedure should be followed but with the mouse pointer on the right indent marker.

Figure 4.7 shows the first paragraph indented from the left and right

Figure 4.7.
Custom
indented
paragraph.

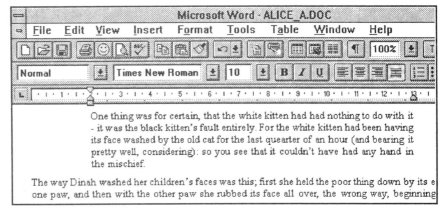

Hanging Indents

The top left triangle - or the *first-line indent marker* allows you to control the first line of a paragraph. This means that you can indent the first line or produce a hanging indent.

With the insertion point still in the first paragraph of the Alice document click on the top triangle and drag it back to the left edge of the ruler. Only the first line of the paragraph is pulled out as can be seen in Figure 4.8.

Figure 4.8.
Using the first-
line indent
marker to create
a hanging indent.

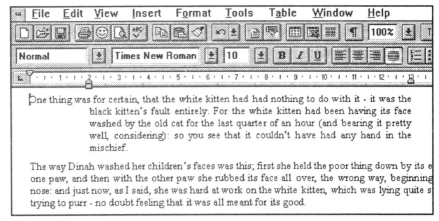

Indenting the First Line

The top triangle can also be used to indent the first line of a paragraph.

1   Place the insertion point somewhere in the second paragraph.

2   Click on the top triangle and drag it in to the 1 inch or 2cm marker.

The first line only of the second paragraph is indented as can be seen in Figure 4.9.

Figure 4.9.
Indenting the first
line only.

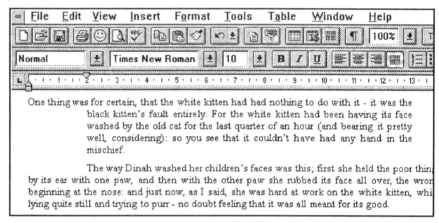

Exercise

1   Re-open the ALICE_1 document and indent the first paragraph by half and inch or 1 cm.

2   Further indent the first line by half a centimetre or a quarter of an inch.

In addition to the options available in the Paragraph dialogue box there are a number of other commands that can be applied to paragraphs, including the creation of numbered lists and bulleted lists, the drawing of borders and shading of text.

Numbered and Bulleted Lists

Two buttons on the Formatting toolbar allow you to quickly assign numbers or bullets to a series of paragraphs to form a list. The format of the numbering and style of the bullets can be adjusted by selecting *Format | Bullets and Numbering*.

Open a new document by clicking on the *New* button on the Standard toolbar.

1 Type in the following pressing ENTER at the end of each line:

Alice

Dinah

Humpty Dumpty

The Cheshire Cat

The White Rabbit

2 Select the first three paragraphs.

3 Click on the *Numbering* button 　.

4 Select the last two paragraphs.

5 Click on the *Bullets* button 　.

Figure 4.10 shows the results.

Figure 4.10.
List with numbers
and bullets.

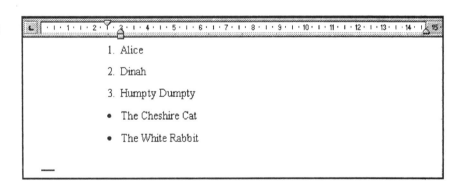

If you want to number non consecutive paragraphs you must first select all paragraphs and click on the *Numbering* button. You can then select those paragraphs that are not to be numbered and click again on *Numbering* button.

1 Click on the second paragraph.

2   Click on the *Numbering* button.

The first paragraph is now number 1 and the third paragraph is number 2.

Both the *Numbering* and the *Bullets* buttons are *toggle* buttons in that the same procedure is used to turn on the feature as is used to turn it off.

To change the style of numbers and bullets select **Format | Bullets and Numbering** which accesses the dialogue box shown in Figure 4.11.

Figure 4.11.
Bullets and
Numbering
dialogue box.

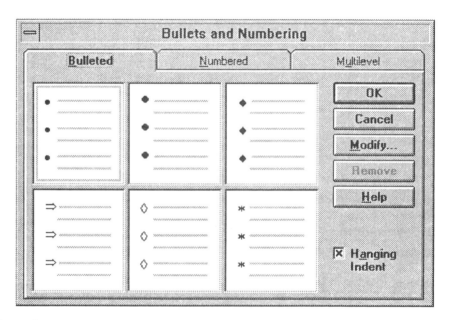

Exercise

1   Remove the bullets and numbering assigned to the above list.

2   Bullet the complete list with heart shaped bullets.

3   Number the list commencing with number 3.

Borders and Shading

Borders or lines may be added to any side of a paragraph, and you can apply background shading to text. Borders and shading are accessed by selecting

Format | Borders and Shading, or to access some of the most commonly used border options, the Borders toolbar can be displayed by clicking on the

Borders button on the Formatting toolbar ⊞. Figure 4.12 shows the Borders toolbar.

Figure 4.12. The Borders toolbar.

To put a ¾ point border on the second paragraph of the ALICE_1 document:

1   Ensure the insertion point is somewhere on the paragraph.

2   Click on the *Outside Border* button ▣. Figure 4.13 shows the results.

Figure 4.13. Full border around a paragraph.

The way Dinah washed her children's faces was this; first she held the poor thing down by its ear with one paw, and then with the other paw she rubbed its face all over, the wrong way, beginning at the nose: and just now, as I said, she was hard at work on the white kitten, which was lying quite still and trying to purr - no doubt feeling that it was all meant for its good.

To shade the paragraph:

1   Click the arrow to the right of the *Shading* box (which says *Clear*)

2   Click on 25%. Figure 4.14 shows the effect of this shading.

Figure 4.14. 25% shading.

The way Dinah washed her children's faces was this; first she held the poor thing down by its ear with one paw, and then with the other paw she rubbed its face all over, the wrong way, beginning at the nose: and just now, as I said, she was hard at work on the white kitten, which was lying quite still and trying to purr - no doubt feeling that it was all meant for its good.

The *Borders and Shading* option on the Format menu provides some further features, including specifying the space between the text and the border.

For example, to leave a 20 point space around the text in the above paragraph:

1   Select Format | Borders and Shading.

2   Click on the up arrow to the right of the From Text box until it reads 20pt. Figure 4.15 shows the results.

*Figure 4.15.
Adjusting the
space between
the text and the
border.*

> The way Dinah washed her children's faces was this; first she
> held the poor thing down by its ear with one paw, and then
> with the other paw she rubbed its face all over, the wrong way,
> beginning at the nose: and just now, as I said, she was hard at
> work on the white kitten, which was lying quite still and trying
> to purr - no doubt feeling that it was all meant for its good.

Exercise

1   Re-open the ALICE_1 document and draw a 3 point horizontal line above and below the first paragraph.

2   Shade the second paragraph with a 30% shading.

3   Hide the Borders toolbar.

Summary

In this chapter you have learnt how to use the Standard and Formatting toolbars to format text in order to present your work in the way you want it as opposed to the way in which it automatically appears when you type in the text. In addition you have seen how entire paragraphs can be formatted using the *Format | Paragraph* commands and you are able to shade text and draw borders around paragraphs.

Self Test

1   What is the shortcut key to put text in italics whilst typing?

2   What determines the range of fonts available for your use in Word?

3   What is required to put all the words in a paragraph in upper case?

4   What does the tOGGLE cASE option on the Change Case dialogue box do?

5   What is the purpose of the Format Painter button on the Standard Toolbar?

6   What is the significance of the paragraph mark and where is it located

7   Suggest two ways of seeing the formatting applied to a paragraph.

8   By how much is a paragraph indented when the *Indent* button is pressed?

9   What is the difference between the square and the upward facing triangle to the left of the horizontal ruler?

10   How can you adjust the spacing between the text and an accompanying border?

FIVE
Proofing Tools

Key Learning Points In This Chapter

- Using the spelling checker
- Using the grammar checker
- Using the thesaurus
- Adjusting hyphenation
- Using word count

Introduction

In addition to the formatting tools discussed in Chapter Four Word provides a number of features that assist in the proofing of a document. These include a spelling checker and grammar checker, a Thesaurus and the ability to customise the way hyphenation is performed. This chapter looks at these features and shows you how to get the most from them.

The file PROOF_A.DOC in Appendix B must be created and saved in the STEPWORD directory in order to complete the exercises in this chapter. You will begin by saving the file with a different name so that you can return to the original at a later stage.

1   Open the file either by clicking on the *Open* button on the Standard toolbar or by selecting *Open* from the File menu.

2   Double-click on the filename to open the document.

3   Save the file with *File | Save As* entering the name **PROOF_1**.

Note: *When you install Word the Setup program gives you the option to install or not install the Word proofing tools, which include the Spelling Checker, the Grammar checker and the Thesaurus. If you do not see these commands on the **Tools** menu you cannot proceed with this chapter until you install them.*

Spelling Checker

The spelling checker compares the spelling of each word with a standard dictionary supplied by Word. You can add words to the dictionary which means you can include technical terms or proper names that you currently use.

Spell checking commences from the insertion point and continues to the end of the file or you can *select* a piece of text that you want to check. To spell check the PROOF_A file ensure the insertion point is at the beginning of the document and click on the *Spelling* button on the Standard toolbar. The dialogue box in Figure 5.1 will be displayed as soon as the spelling checker finds a word that is not in the dictionary.

Tip: *A quick way to get the insertion point to the beginning of a document from anywhere within it is to press* CTRL+HOME.

Figure 5.1.
Spelling dialogue
box.

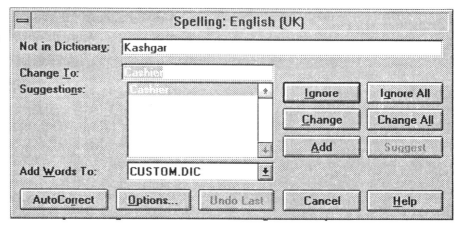

The first word that has been picked up is 'Kashgar, which is the name of a place and is correctly spelt. As this is not likely to be required again, either the *Ignore* or the *Ignore All* button is required. If you think the word might appear again later in this document then you should click *Ignore All* which will prevent the spell checker stopping the next time this word occurs. However, if you want the spelling check to stop if it finds the word again you should click on *Ignore*. For this example, click on *Ignore All*.

Proceed through the document and respond as indicated below.

And   First suggestion of 'and' is correct. This is a mistake you often tend to make so it should be included in the *AutoCorrect* list. Click the *AutoCorrect* button which will change this and any other occurrences of the error and will add the word to the *AutoCorrect* list.

floowing   First suggestion is correct so click on *Change*

Yangtze   You intend writing more on this river so it is worth adding it to the dictionary. Click on the *Add* button.

deevides   Second suggestion is required, click on 'divides' and then click on *Change*.

the the	Repeated word. The *Change* button now reads *Delete*. Click this to remove one instance of 'the'.
andsilk	No suggestion offered. Click in the *Change To* box, move the insertion point to before the 's' and press SPACE. Click *Change*.
southwestern	Suggests the word should be hyphenated. Accept by clicking *Change*.
neolithic	Suggests the word should be capitalised. Accept by clicking *Change*.
Stendalton	No suggestions. The word is correctly spelt and you want to use this name again so it should be added to the dictionary. Click on the *Add* button.

When the spell checking is complete click on the *OK* button.

Spelling Options

You can control the way Word checks spelling by clicking the *Options* button on the Spelling dialogue box, or by selecting the *Spelling* tab from the *Tools | Options* dialogue box. This is shown in Figure 5.2.

Figure 5.2. Spelling Options dialogue box.

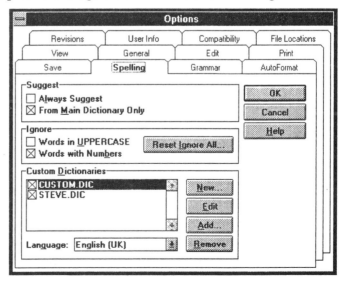

These options allow you to fine tune the way the spelling check works for you. For example, *Always Suggest* means that the system will always list alternative words to choose from when an unrecognised word is found. If you switch this off then the checker will identify that a word is incorrectly spelt, but you will then have to click the *Suggest* box on the Spelling dialogue box to get the list. Switching off this option will speed up spell checking, especially if you have a lot of words to which you will reply *Ignore* because you do not have to wait whilst the system searches for likely correct words each time.

The *Ignore* section of the Spelling Options dialogue box allow you to ignore words in capital letters or words that contain numbers. The *Reset Ignore All* button is important. When you complete a spell Word remembers the words you said *Ignore All* to and will continue to ignore those words on any other document you might spell check during the current session with Word. There might be occasions when you need to pick up words in another document that were ignored in the current one and therefore the *Reset Ignore All* button should be clicked.

Customised Dictionaries

If you regularly use technical terms, acronyms or proper names you should use a custom dictionary to check their spelling. Word supplies a default custom dictionary into which words you *Add* during a spelling check are automatically placed. In addition, you can create your own dictionaries which can be applied to different documents. You can also purchase special dictionaries such as foreign languages, medical or legal terms etc.

Note: *If you have a number of different custom dictionaries make sure that the correct one is selected before you spell check a document.*

Dictionaries are just text files with a DIC extension and can be deleted or edited at any time. To edit a dictionary highlight it on the list in the spelling options dialogue box and then select *Edit* which will open the dictionary as a normal Word document. You can then add, delete or edit text in the file. When you save the file make sure it is stored as a *text-only* file.

Checking Grammar

The Grammar check facility in Word identifies sentences that contain possible grammatical or stylistic errors and offers you ways of improvement. In addition, unless you switch the feature off, the grammar check will also check spelling.

There are three 'rule groups' by which Word analyses the grammar of a document. These are formal, business and casual. For this document casual is the most appropriate.

1 Select *Tools | Options* and click the *Grammar* tab to access the Grammar Options dialogue box as shown in Figure 5.3.

Figure 5.3.
Grammar Options
Dialogue Box

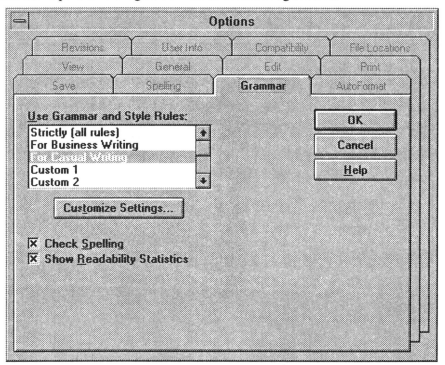

2 Select *For Casual Writing* from the list and then click OK

To check the grammar of the PROOF_A document, re-open the original PROOF_A document and ensure the insertion point is at the beginning of the file.

1   Select *Tools | Grammar* .

2   The Grammar dialogue box is displayed when a sentence that could be improved is identified. In this example the word Kashgar will be picked up as a misspelled word first. Select *Ignore* from the Spelling dialogue box and then the Grammar dialogue box will be displayed as shown in Figure 5.4.

Figure 5.4.
Grammar
dialogue box.

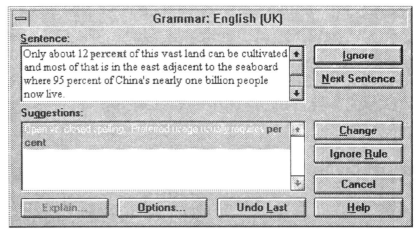

Although 'percent' is not an incorrect spelling the grammar check suggests that the preferred usage is two words, per cent.

3   Select *Change* to accept the suggestion.

4   Correct the spelling and observe the suggestions made by the grammar check for the remainder of the document.

Note: *Use the Explain button if you do not understand the suggested problem with the sentence.*

If a particular suggestion keeps appearing and you want to ignore it, click on the *Ignore Rule* button.

Thesaurus

The Word thesaurus provides synonyms, and sometimes antonyms, for a particular word. In addition it provides lists of related words and different forms for the selected word. For example, the word "race" can be both a noun and a verb; the thesaurus provides synonyms for both forms.

You use the thesaurus to find an alternative for a particular word. Before proceeding type in the following sentence.

Information technology is changing more prolifically than ever before. Managers are requiring more expertise in order to manage their departments efficiently.

The word 'more' has been repeated in this sentence and the thesaurus can help find an alternative word.

1 Highlight the second 'more'.

2 Select *Tools | Thesaurus* and Figure 5.5 shows the resulting dialogue box.

*Figure 5.5.
Thesaurus
dialogue box.*

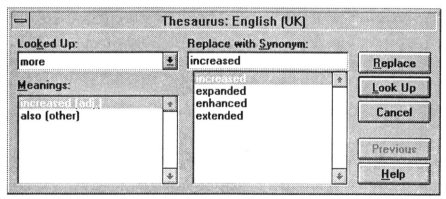

3 The first suggested synonym of 'increased' is a good alternative in this case and so click the Replace button to change the word.

In the above sentence the use of the words 'Manager' and 'manages' does not read well.

1 Highlight 'manage'.
2 Select *Tools | Thesaurus*.

3 The suggested replacements are not suitable because the first meaning of the word 'manage' has been listed as 'achieve'. In this case 'direct' is the meaning we require. Click on 'direct' and the *Replace* list changes. Figure 5.6 shows the resulting dialogue box.

Figure 5.6. Changing the meaning of a word.

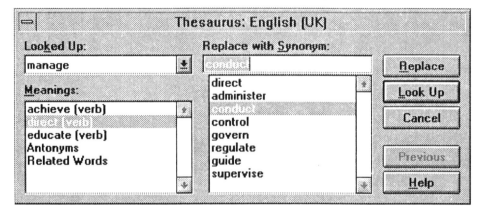

4 Select 'supervise' as the word to replace 'manage'.

If you don't see a word that you want to use you can click on the *Look Up* button which would, in the above example, then look up the word 'direct' and give you a list of suggested replacements.

Hyphenation

The use of hyphenation can reduce the ragged appearance of unjustified text, thus allowing you to fit more text on the page. When working with justified text, hyphenation can reduce the 'white space' between words which is especially evident when working with narrow columns.

Hyphenation is managed through the Hyphenation dialogue box which is accessed by selecting *Tools | Hyphenation*. Figure 5.7 shows the resulting dialogue box.

Automatic Hyphenation

1 Re-open the PROOF_A document
2 Select *Tools | Hyphenation.*
3 Check the *Automatically Hyphenate Document* box and click *OK*.

*Figure 5.7.
Hyphenation
dialogue box.*

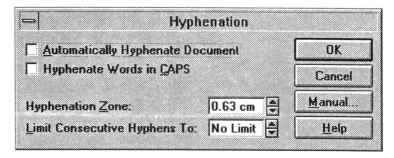

The *Hyphenation Zone* allows you to specify the amount of space that can be left between the end of the last word on a line and the right margin. This space determines whether or not a word will be hyphenated. The wider you make this zone the fewer hyphens you will have. However if you are working with left justified text you can reduced the raggedness by making the hyphenation zone smaller and including more hyphenation.

The *Limit Consecutive Hyphens To* box allows you to select the number of consecutive lines that can be hyphenated.

If you have a particular paragraph in a document that you do not want to be hyphenated you can select *Format | Paragraph | Text Flow* and check the *Don't Hyphenate* box.

If you decide that you do not want the document to be hyphenated, clear the *Automatically Hyphenate Document* box and click *OK*. All the hyphens that were automatically inserted will be removed.

Manual Hyphenation

Re-open the PROOF_A document.

1   Select **Tools | Hyphenation**.

2   Do not check the *Automatic* button (or clear it if necessary).

3   Click *Manual*.

The first word to be hyphenated is displayed and you have the option to accept the suggested hyphenation point by clicking *Yes* or to move it to a different part of the word before clicking *Yes*.

To skip the word without hyphenating it click *No.* You can also stop hyphenation part way through the document by clicking *Cancel.*

Tip: *If you use the hyphenation command manually you should wait until you have finished editing your document as adding or deleting text will affect the way lines break.*

Nonbreaking and Optional Hyphens

When you are entering text you can specify nonbreaking and optional hyphens. A nonbreaking hyphen is used when you do not want a hyphenated word to break across two lines.

For example, to ensure the word 'mother-in-law' always stays on the same line, nonbreaking hyphens must be used.

Type: **Mother**
          CTRL+SHIFT+ **– (hyphen)**
          In
          CTRL+SHIFT+ **– (hyphen)**
          Law

An optional hyphen is used when you want to specify where the hyphen should be positioned if it is required.

For example, if you want the word 'consideration' to be 'consid-eration' if it comes at the end of a line a soft hyphen is placed after the 'd' .

Type: **consid**
          CTRL+ **– (hyphen)**
          eration

Word Count

When proofing and editing it may be useful to see how many words or characters, lines or paragraphs the document, or part of the document, is in length. The *Word Count* option on the Tools menu is used for this purpose.

1 Re-open the PROOF_A document

2 Select *Tools* | *Word Count*

Figure 5.8.
Word Count
dialogue box.

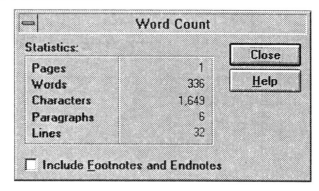

You can select any amount of text before selecting *Tools* | *Word Count* and then only your selection will be counted.

Summary

In this chapter you have seen how to check the accuracy of your document in terms of spelling and grammar. However, it is important to remember that these tools are only an aid to document proofing and there is no substitute for carefully reading the document for complete accuracy.

Self Test

1 From what point does spell checking commence?

2 How do you begin a spelling check?

3 When is the Spelling dialogue box first displayed?

4 What is the difference between the *Ignore* and the *Ignore All* buttons on the Spelling dialogue box?

5 What does the *Reset Ignore All* button on the Spelling Options dialogue box do?

6 What file extension does a dictionary file have?

7   What is a 'rule group' when referring to the Grammar checker?

8   How do you specify the required 'rule group'.

9   What does the *Look Up* button on the Thesaurus dialogue box do?

10   What is the difference between a nonbreaking hyphen and an optional hyphen?

SIX
Printing Documents

Key Learning Points In The Chapter

- Print a document using the Print menu and the Print button

- Print selected pages and sections of a document

- Use Print Preview to view longer documents

- Optimise document appearance from within Print Preview

Introduction

Two files will be used in this chapter in order to practice the Print features of Word. Initially the ALICE_1 document that you created in Chapter Three will be opened and printed. You will then need to have a longer document available which will be used to illustrate the *Print | Preview* command and the pagination options available.

Printing a Document

Documents in Word must first be opened before they can be printed.

1   Using the *Open* button, ensure that the STEPWORD directory is current and open the file ALICE_1.

Printing can be initiated either by clicking on the *Print* button or by selecting *File | Print*.

2   To print the ALICE_1 document on the default printer, click on the *Print* button and the file will be printed directly.

There are no messages or prompts when the *Print* button is used and the whole document will always be printed. If you look at the status line at the bottom of the screen when you click on the *Print* button you will see some dots displayed. This indicates that the file is being copied to the Windows Print Manager from where the printing takes place in background mode. Once the file has been copied to Print Manager (which will be very quick with this small file), you can continue working in Word and you can even start another print job.

Print the same ALICE_1 document again, but using the Print dialogue box.

3   Select *File | Print* which will produce the dialogue box shown in Figure 6.1.

Figure 6.1.
Print dialogue
box.

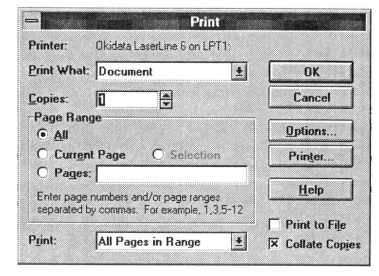

The printer that is listed in this box is the default printer that is established when setting up Windows. This printer choice may be changed by clicking on *Printer* in the Print dialogue box which will display the available printers as may be seen in Figure 6.2. It is important to ensure that your computer is connected, either directly or through the network, to the printer you choose to use. In most cases, if your system has been set up correctly the default printer will be the correct choice.

Figure 6.2.
Print Setup
dialogue box.

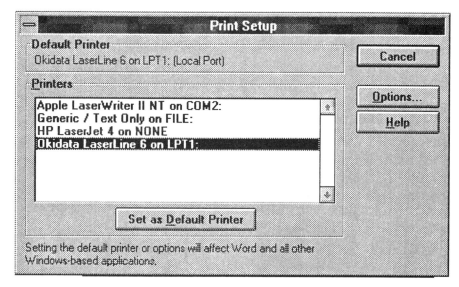

The other sections of the print dialogue box allow you to specify how many copies you wish to print and what part of the document you want. The default selection is to print one copy of the entire document, but you can choose to print the current page or a selection of pages. In addition you can highlight a range before selecting *File | Print* and print that selection.

4 In the first instance the default settings are all correct to it is only necessary to either press ENTER or click *OK* to commence printing the ALICE_1 document.

Printing Selected Parts of a Document

In order to see the benefits of some of the other printing options, open any Word file that is at least three pages long, such as SAMPLE6.DOC in the \WINWORD\WORBCBT directory. The example used in the following explanation is a three page document, the opening screen of which may be seen in Figure 6.3.

Figure 6.3. Beginning of a three page document.

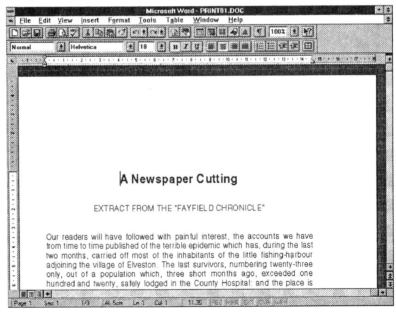

Access the Print dialogue box by selecting *File | Print*. You can now specify which pages of the document you wish to print together with the number of copies required. For example, to print two copies of the first page (which should be the current page as it is where the insertion point is located),

1 Click on *Current Page*.

2 Click on the up arrow to the right of the number of copies box until 2 is displayed.

3 Click on *OK* to print the pages.

To print one copy of pages 1 and 2.

1 Select *File | Print*.

2 Click on *Pages*.

3 Enter **1-2** at the insertion point.

4 Click on *OK* to print the pages.

If you want to print pages 1 and 3, follow the above steps, but in the page range box type 1,3. Any number of specific pages may be printed by separating each page with a comma. A combination of ranges and specific pages can also be entered. For example, 1-4,6,8,10-13 would be a valid entry in the print range box.

It is also possible to select a range within the document to be printed. For example, to print the second paragraph of the document,

1 Highlight the paragraph to select it.

2 Select *File | Print*.

3 Click on *Selection*.

4 Click *OK* to print the selected range.

Note: *The Selection option in the Print dialogue box is only available if a range has been selected. If you are trying to print an entire document and only a small range is printed, check to see if you had a range highlighted when you accessed the Print command.*

Print Preview

In order to see how the document will look when it is printed you can use the *Print Preview* window. This allows the overall appearance of one or more pages to be seen. Although it is hard to read the text in most cases, you can see where the text falls on the page in relation to margins and page breaks.

Tip: *Taking the time to preview a document can ultimately save time by reducing the number of times you need to print a file before getting the layout absolutely correct.*

Print Preview may be accessed either by clicking on the *Print Preview* button or by selecting *File | Print Preview*. Figure 6.4 shows how the PRINT_A document will appear on accessing Print Preview. The current page is displayed, which in the case of Figure 6.4 is the first page of the document. There is a toolbar with the buttons that can be used whilst in Print Preview, but the menu bar has not changed.

Figure 6.4.
Print Preview.

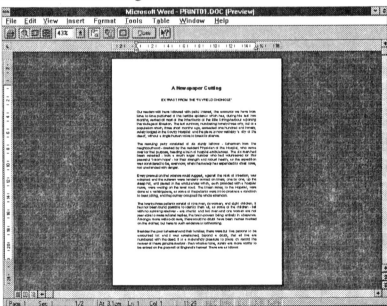

In Figure 6.4 you will notice that the document is displayed at 43% of it's actual size. This can be adjusted by clicking on the arrow to the left of the *Size* button. In addition to selecting a range of percentage sizes there are also options to display the document at a size that will fit across the page width, to display two pages or one whole page.

In addition the *Full Page* button removes the Main Menu and Standard toolbar from the screen, leaving more space to view the document. This is especially useful when working with large pages. The *Full Page* button is a toggle button which means that when you non longer want the view your document in this way you click on the button again and the display is returned to the default and the menus are returned.

Previewing Multiple Pages

Multiple pages can be viewed together on the screen by using the *Multiple Pages* button on the *Print Preview* toolbar. Clicking on this button displays a series of pages which vary according to the length of the document and the size you wish to view the pages. With longer documents you will be able to see more pages on the screen by reducing the size using the *Size* button. In the case of the example file, Figure 6.5 shows what appears on clicking the *Multiple Pages* button.

*Figure 6.5.
Multiple pages
button.*

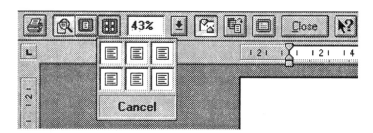

To display the three pages of the document drag the mouse over the top three boxes. The result is shown in Figure 6.6. You can also determine the layout of the pages on the screen by the pages you select using the *Multiple Pges* button. For example, you could display the three pages two across and one below by dragging across the top two pages and down one row.

Figure 6.6.
Print Preview
with multiple
pages.

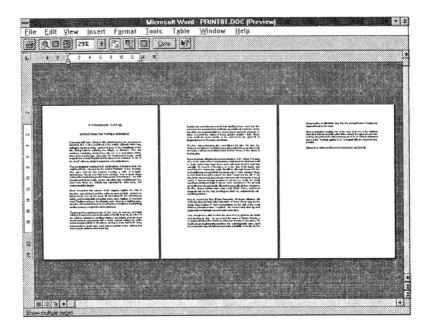

To the left of the *Multiple Page* button on the Print Preview toolbar is the *One Page* button [image] which will return the display to the current page only.

Reducing Document Length

Page three of the document is not very long so it is possible to shrink the font size in order that the text will fit on two pages. This is achieved by clicking on the *Shrink to Fit* button [image]. Clicking on this button once will shrink the document down to two pages. If you are not happy with the reduced size document, you can select *Edit | Undo* from the main menu whilst still in Print Preview and this will return the text to its original size.

Changing Margins in Print Preview

In some cases it might be preferable to change the margin sizes, either instead of reducing the font size, or in addition to this, in order to optimise the appearance of the document. Margins can be changed using *File | Page Layout*, but they can also be adjusted from within Print Preview.

The example document currently has left and right margins of 3.5cm and top and bottom margins of 5cm. Reducing the top and bottom margins by 2cm will bring the document onto two pages.

Whilst in Print Preview and with one page only being viewed,

1 Display the rulers if they are not already on the screen by clicking on the *View Rulers* button 🔲 on the Print Preview toolbar.

2 Move the mouse pointer into the vertical ruler area until it changes to a double arrow shape.

3 Position the pointer near the top edge of the vertical ruler (where the shading changes).

4 Hold down the ALT key and then click and drag the margin up by 2cm.

5 Position the pointer near the bottom edge of the vertical ruler.

6 Hold down the ALT key and then click and drag the margin down by 2cm.

7 Click the *Multiple Pages* button to display three pages and notice that the document now only requires two pages.

Tip: *It is not necessary to use* ALT *key whilst dragging, but displaying the actual measurements on the page is useful when setting margins.*

Editing from within Print Preview

If you notice that a change needs to be made to your document whilst in Print Preview, it is not necessary to return to normal viewing to make the change, as editing can be performed within the Print Preview window.

It is usually preferable to display one page of the document as opposed to multiple pages.

1 Display the page you want to edit and click on the part of the page the change is required. Notice that as you move onto the text the mouse pointer changes to a magnifying glass and when you click that part of the page is magnified on the screen.

2   Click the *Magnifier* button on the Print Preview toolbar which changes the pointer to the I-beam.

3   Click where the editing is required and make the necessary changes.

4   To return the screen to the display prior to editing click again on the *Magnifier* button.

Printing the Document

Having used the Print Preview commands to optimise the appearance of the

document the *Print* button on the Print Preview toolbar may be used to print the whole document. If you want to change any of the print settings then use *File | Print.*

Note: *If you want to retain your document with the changes made with Print Preview, remember to save the file before closing it. If you are changing margins etc. just for printing beware of AutoSave which could save the file with changes that you do not want to retain.*

Exercise

1   Open any Word document of three pages or more.

2   Print the entire document using the *Print* button on the Standard Toolbar.

3   Print two copies of pages 1 and 3 of the document.

4   Using the *Print Preview* tools reduce the left and right margins by 1cm.

5   Using the *Print Preview* tools shrink the document to fit onto two pages.

Summary

In this chapter you have learnt how to print documents in their entirety and by selecting pages and parts of files. The Print Preview window is a useful feature that enables you to tailor the appearance of your document on the screen before you print it. Being able to adjust margins and font sizes through Print Preview can save you time.

Self Test

1   Suggest two ways of printing the entire document.

2   What is required to print pages 2 and 6 of a document?

3   How can you print one paragraph of a document?

4   What is the quickest way to access Print Preview?

5   What is the purpose of the ALT key when adjusting margins?

6   What is required to view six pages of a document?

7   How can you shrink a document to fit on fewer pages from within Print Preview?

8   Having viewed multiple pages how can you return to a single page?

9   How do you change the percentage size of the document on the screen from within Print Preview?

10   How can you edit the document while in Print Preview?

SEVEN
Working with Styles

Key Learning Points In This Chapter

- Creating and applying character styles
- Applying standard styles
- Creating and applying paragraph styles
- Amending styles
- Using AutoFormat

Introduction

When you type text into Word each paragraph is assigned a *style*, the default of which is called *Normal*. You can see this displayed to the left of the Formatting toolbar. However when you are working on a document you might want to indent certain paragraphs, or put certain references in italic etc. Instead of performing the formatting each time it is required you can use either the standard styles supplied by Word, or you can set up your own styles which you can then assign to your text as necessary. In this chapter you will learn the difference between *character* and *paragraph* styles and how to set up and modify them.

Create the file called STYLE_A.DOC from Appendix B and save it in the STEPWORD directory.

1 Click on the *Open* button.

2 Change to the STEPWORD directory if necessary.

3 Double click on STYLE_A.

Save this file with a new name so that the changes you make will not overwrite the original.

4 Select *File | Save As*.

5 In the *File Name* box, type **STYLE_01.**

6 Press ENTER or click the *OK* box.

To see the list of styles available in this document you can click on the arrow to the right of the Style box on the Formatting toolbar. This list consists of the character and paragraph styles currently in use and one or two other pre-defined styles that Word considers you may commonly require. Paragraph styles are displayed in bold, whilst character styles are not in bold. To see a list of all the available styles that Word provides hold down the SHIFT key and click on the arrow to the right of the Style box. You will have to use the scrollbar to see the full list. Figure 7.1 shows the basic list that will be displayed when you click the arrow without holding SHIFT. The highlighted item indicates the paragraph style for the paragraph on which the insertion point is currently located.

Figure 7.1.
Style list.

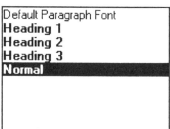

Default Paragraph Font
Heading 1
Heading 2
Heading 3
Normal

Character Styles

When preparing a document it is often necessary to highlight certain pieces of text in the same way so that they stand out. In Chapter Three you learnt how to use the bold, italic and underline buttons to change the appearance of selected text. However, if the same formatting is required repetitively in a document it is more efficient to create a *character style* that can be assigned to any selected text.

Creating a Character Style

The STYLE_01 document is an outline for a training course on Microsoft Windows. To highlight the word 'Windows' each time it appears by having it in bold italic, a style can be created.

The first step is to set the required formatting,

1   Select "**Windows**" in the first line of the introduction by double clicking on the word.

2   Click the *Bold* and *Italic* buttons on the Formatting toolbar.

With the word still highlighted a character style can be established.

3   Select *Format | Style* which will produce the dialogue box in Figure 7.2.

*Figure 7.2.
Style dialogue
box.*

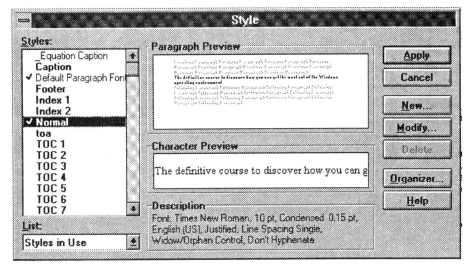

4   Click the *New* button to create a new style which will produce the
dialogue box in Figure 7.3

*Figure 7.3.
New Style
dialogue box.*

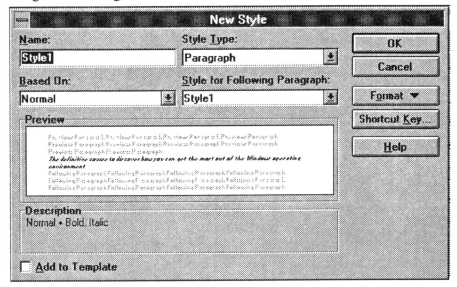

5   In the *Name* box, type BOLDITAL.

Note: *A style name may be up to 255 characters in length and may
contain spaces, letters and numbers. Two styles cannot have the same
name, but Word does differentiate between upper and lower case.*

6   Click on the arrow to the right of the *Style Type* box and select Character.

7   Click *OK* which will return you to the original Style dialogue box.

Notice that BOLDITAL has been added to the list of styles and that it is not in bold. Paragraph styles are always displayed in bold and character styles not in bold.

8   Click the *Apply* button to apply the style to your selected text and to return to the document.

Applying A Character Style

The Window style can now be assigned to any selected text.

1   Select the word "**Windows**" on the second line.

2   Click on the arrow to the right of the *Style* box on the Formatting toolbar.

3   Select the style BOLDITAL.

The style is applied to the selected text and you are returned to the document.

You can now proceed through the document selecting all occurrences of the word "Windows" and assign it the style BOLDITAL.

Tip: *Pressing the* F4 *function key repeats the last operation and so instead of having to select BOLDITAL from the Style box each time you can highlight the next occurrence of the word "Windows" and press* F4.

Note: *If you format a selection of text and then decide that you don't like it you can return to the default style for that paragraph by holding down the* CTRL *key and pressing* SPACEBAR *or by selecting Default Paragraph Font from the Style Box.*

Assigning a Keyboard Shortcut

If you are going to use a character style regularly it is useful to assign the style a short-cut key which speeds up the application of the style on selected text.

1   Select *Format | Style*.

2   Click on the BOLDITAL style.

3   Click on the *Modify* button and then click on the *Shortcut Key* button in the next dialogue box.

4   With the insertion point in the *Press New Shortcut Key* box, press CTRL+SHIFT+E.

Note: *When selecting a combination to use for the shortcut key notice that below the typing area Word will display whether your chosen combination is currently assigned to something else or, as in the case of* CTRL+SHIFT+E, *is unassigned. You can change the use of existing shortcut keys if you wish.*

5   Click the *Assign* button which assigns this key combination to the character style BOLDITAL.

6   Close the dialogue boxes to return to the document.

To use the shortcut key select some text in the STYLE_01 document and press CTRL+SHIFT+E.

Exercise

1   Create a character style called BOLD which consists of bold text.

2   Apply the style to the first two words of each line in the "**What You Will Learn**" section.

3   Return the formatted text to the normal paragraph text.

Paragraph Styles

A paragraph style allows you to format a paragraph exactly as you want it and then apply the format to any other paragraph. This means that in addition to specifying how the text will appear you can define the alignment and spacing for the paragraph.

Tip: *Paragraph styles are stored in the paragraph marker at the end of a paragraph and it is advisable to show these markers when working with paragraph styles in order not to mistakenly delete a marker and all the formatting that goes with it.*

Word Paragraph Styles

Word provides a series of predefined styles for all documents. *Normal* represents the standard paragraph style used when entering text. Figure 7.4 shows the current settings for the *Normal* paragraph style. The *Default Paragraph Font* is the standard character style. The headings styles provide three levels of topic headings and the two envelope styles are for use when preparing envelopes.

Figure 7.4.
The Normal
paragraph style.

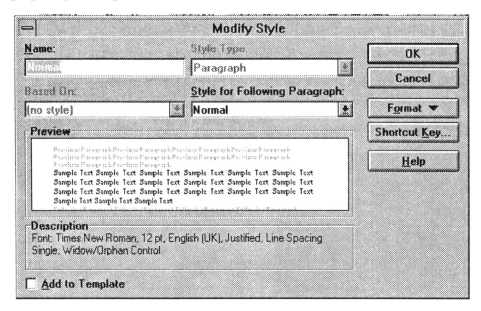

Creating User-Defined Paragraph Styles

It is possible to create a paragraph style using the *Style* option from the Format menu in much the same way as a character style. However, a more efficient method is to use the *Style* box on the Formatting toolbar. The following steps will create a paragraph style for the headings in the STYLE_01 document.

1 Select the word "**Introduction**" on the second line. Make sure this is selected as a paragraph by clicking once in the margin to the left of the word.

2 Click the *Bold* button and increase the font size to 16 point.

3 Click on the currently displayed style, Normal, in the *Style* box on the Formatting toolbar.

4 Type in **NEWHEAD** as the style name which will replace Normal and press ENTER.

If you select the paragraph now you will notice that the name in the *Style* box on the Formatting toolbar is NEWHEAD.

A shortcut key can be assigned to a paragraph style in the same way as character styles. Word has automatically assigned a shortcut key for the Normal paragraph style which is CTRL+SHIFT+N.

Applying a Paragraph Style

1 Scroll down the STYLE_01 document to the next heading which is "**What You Will Learn**".

2 Select the paragraph by clicking in the left margin.

3 Click on the arrow to the right of the *Style* box which will list the available styles. Notice that Word provides some standard styles such as Heading 1, Heading 2 etc.

4 Select the NEWHEAD style.

The format is applied to the paragraph.

Note: *If you format a paragraph and then wish to return it to the Normal style you can either select the paragraph and then choose Normal from the Style Box, or you can press* CTRL+SHIFT+N.

Exercise

1 Using the "**What You Will Learn**" section create a paragraph style called INDENT in which the left and right margins are indented by 1 cm (or half an inch).

2 Apply the format to all the paragraphs in this section and to the "**Documentation**" section.

3 Return the "**Documentation**" section to the Normal style.

Redefining a Style

On occasions it is necessary to redefine a paragraph style and for the changes to be reflected on all paragraphs using that style. This is achieved by selecting a paragraph of the format to be changed, making the necessary changes and then redefining the style.

To illustrate this the paragraph style NEWHEAD will be changed so that the text is 18 point and the text of the paragraph will be put into italics.

1 Select the first paragraph with the NEWHEAD style.

2 Increase the font size to 18 points.

3 Click on the *Italic* button on the Formatting toolbar.

4 With the paragraph still selected click on the style name in the *Style* box. and the dialogue box shown in Figure 7.5 will be displayed.

*Figure 7.5.
Redefining a
style.*

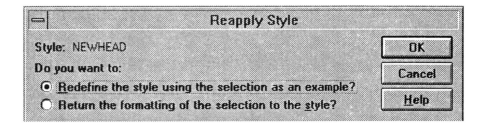

5   Make sure the first option is selected and click *OK*.
All the paragraphs with the NEWHEAD style name will be changed to the
new format.

Note: *Character styles can be changed in the same way.*

Tip: *If you want to create a new style that is similar to an existing one, select
the closest style from the Based On box in the New Style dialogue box.*

Exercise

1   Change the paragraph style INDENT created in the previous
exercise so that the left margin is indented by 2cms or 1 inch..

2   Create a new style based on INDENT in which the text is italics.

Using AutoFormat

After typing text into a document you can use the built-in AutoFormat
command to have Word format the text for you. Word analyses each
paragraph currently formatted with the *Normal* style and decides whether it
is a heading, part of a bulleted list, body text, and so on. Word then applies
an appropriate style. Paragraphs formatted with other styles will not be
changed.

AutoFormat can also improve a document with the following features where
appropriate.

• Remove additional hard returns at the end of each line of body text.

- Replace straight quotation marks and apostrophes (" and ') with smart quotes (" " and ' ').

- Replace "(C)", "(R)" and "(TM)" with ©, ®, and ™.

- Replace asterisks, hyphens, or other characters used for bulleted lists with a bullet character.

- Indent paragraphs to replace horizontal spacing inserted by using TAB or the SPACEBAR.

To see the effect of the AutoFormat command:

1   Open the original STYLE_A.DOC file and save it as STYLE_02.DOC.

2   With the insertion point at the beginning of the document select *File | AutoFormat* and click *OK* to commence the procedure.

3   For this exercise click on *Accept* when the dialogue box appears.

If you scroll through the document you will notice that AutoFormat has applied the Heading 1 style to the main heading and Heading 2 to the sub-headings. The dashes that preceded the list under 'What You Will Learn' have been converted to bullets and the paragraphs have been properly spaced. The spacing between paragraphs has been improved so that the extra paragraph markers could be removed.

If you don't like everything that AutoFormat has done you can choose to *Review Changes* which enables you to reject those formats you do not want to use. Alternatively you can choose *Style Gallery* which allows you to apply formats from a different template. Because Word uses standard style names such as Heading 1 and Heading 2 in every template it is easy to apply styles from any template to any document through the AutoFormat command. See Chapter Eight for more about Templates.

Tip: *You can use AutoFormat on a selected piece of text. Highlight the text to format and then choose AutoFormat from the Format menu.*

Exercise

1	Re-open the original STYLE_A document and save it under a different name such as STYLE_03.
2	Use the AutoFormat command to format the document and then use the Style Gallery option to apply the formats from the LETTER1 template.

Summary

In this chapter you have learnt how to create, apply and change character and paragraph styles. Through the use of styles, Word makes it easy for you to format your documents exactly as you want them with continuity of style, both in terms of fonts used, as well as how paragraphs are aligned, spaced etc.

Self Test

1   How can you see the styles supplied by Word?

2   What is the difference between a character style and a paragraph style?

3   How do you identify a Character Style from the list of styles in the style box?

4   What does the F4 function key do?

5   How can you return text formatted with a character style to the Default Paragraph Font?

6   How do you assign a shortcut key to an existing paragraph style?

7   What is the shortcut key combination to return a paragraph style to Normal?

8   What effect does redefining a paragraph style have on the rest of the document?

9   How do you access the AutoFormat command?

10   What do you have to do to apply styles from a different template when using AutoFormat?

EIGHT
Wizards and Templates

Key Learning Points In This Chapter

- Using a wizard to create a letter

- Produce an envelope

- Create a new template

- Create a document based on the new template

Introduction

Word supplies a number of facilities to speed up the creation of documents by performing various formatting procedures for you. This is mainly achieved in two ways; through the use of *wizards* and *templates*.

Both wizards and templates are files stored in the Template sub-directory of the Winword directory. Wizard files have an extension of *WIZ* whilst template files have an extension of *DOT*. Although you can create your own template files, Word supplies a large number which allow you to work with a wide range of different document types.

Wizards prompt you to specify what sort of styles and formatting you require for a document, whilst templates have all the styles and formatting preset so that you can begin work on the document directly. For example, this book has been written using Word and a template was created with all the formatting requirements so that each chapter, which is a separate file, has the same formatting and styles available without having to recreate them.

Wizards

A wizard file guides you through the process of creating a document by prompting you to answer questions about the style and other formatting options you want. Each wizard file is designed to help you create a different type of document. The wizard files supplied with Word are:-

> Agenda Wizard
> Award Wizard
> Calendar Wizard
> CV Wizard
> Fax Wizard
> Letter Wizard
> Memo Wizard
> Newslttr Wizard
> Table Wizard

As you can see the names speak for themselves. In this chapter the Letter Wizard will be used to create a customised letter.

Loading A Wizard

1   Ensure you are in Normal View by clicking the left *View* icon at the bottom of the screen.

2   Select *File | New* which will display the New dialogue box shown in Figure 8.1.

Figure 8.1.
The New
dialogue box.

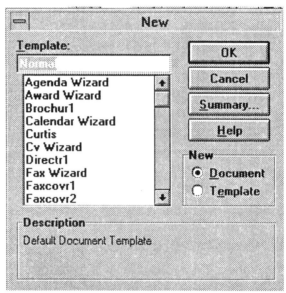

This dialogue box lists all the available templates and wizards.

1   Scroll through the list and select *Letter Wizard.*

2   Click *OK* or press ENTER to load the file.

After a short delay whilst the letter wizard is being loaded, the first window appears as shown in Figure 8.2.

As you can see there are three different types of letter that can be produced using the Letter Wizard. For this exercise a business letter will be created.

Figure 8.2.
First window of
letter wizard.

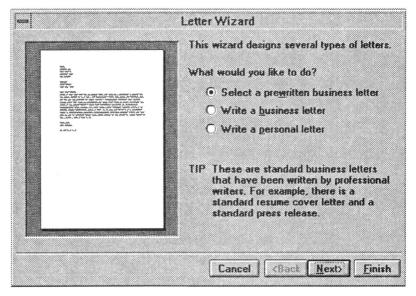

Answering Wizard Questions

1 Select the *Write a business letter* option

2 Click the *Next* button to proceed to the next screen which is shown in Figure 8.3.

Figure 8.3.
Options for letter
wizard.

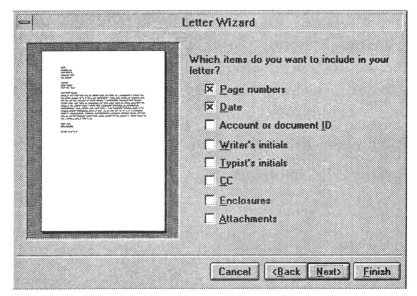

3   Select the *Date* and *Enclosures* boxes and clear any other checked boxes.

4   Click the *Next* button to proceed to the next dialogue box.

5   Select the *Letterhead* option and click *Next* to proceed.

6   Select *At top* and make the margin measurement 5cms.

7   Click the *Next* button to move the next dialogue box.

8   Delete any existing text in the top right box and fill in the addressees details as follows: (remember to press ENTER at the end of each line)

Sarah Hutchinson
Marketing Manager
PC Solutions Ltd
Melbourne Road
Liverpool
L61 3PJ

9   Press TAB to move the return address box.

10 Delete the existing text and enter the following:

Patricia Fellows
PC Consultants Ltd
54 High Street
Weybridge
WE23 5AS

11 Check for any mistakes before proceeding by clicking on the *Next* button.

12 Choose the *Contemporary* option and click *Next* to proceed to the next dialogue box.

13 Select *Create an envelope or mailing label* and then click the *Finish* button.

The Envelopes and Labels dialogue box appears as shown in Figure 8.4

Figure 8.4.
Envelopes and
Labels dialogue
box.

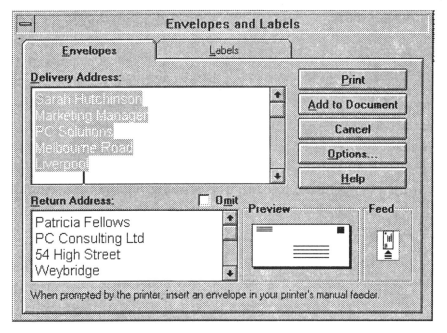

14 Click the *Add To Document* button

This ensures that an envelope is printed each time you print the letter. It will print first and you will be prompted to insert an envelope into the manual feeder of your printer.

15 Click the *No* button is response to whether you want the return address information to be saved as the default.

Type the Letter

The areas into which you are expected to enter your text are showing inside square brackets. In this example the first text entry required is the recipient.

1 Select the word "[**Recipient**]" together with the square brackets.

2 Type **Sarah**.

3 Select "[**Type the body of your letter here**]" and enter the body of the letter as follows:

I need you to update last month's sales figures to take account of the new business we acquired in Brussels. I enclose the current figures for your reference. Could you send me an updated report as soon as possible so that I can forward it to George.

Notice that whilst in Normal View there are a series of small squares before the paragraph marker on the blank lines between the Sincerely and Enclosures. These blank lines are where you will sign the letter and put your name and title. The small squares indicate that these lines cannot be separated by a page break

1   Move the insertion point two lines below 'Sincerely'.

2   Type **Patricia Fellows**.

3   Select the brackets and text after the word 'Enclosures' and type **1**.

The completed letter may be seen in Figure 8.5.

*Figure 8.5.
Completed letter.*

```
22·April·1994¶

¶
▪ Sarah·Hutchinson¶
▪ Marketing·Manager¶
▪ PC·Solutions¶
▪ Melbourne·Road¶
▪ Liverpool¶
▪ L60·6AJ¶


¶

Dear·Sarah¶

I·need·you·to·update·last·month's·sales·figures·to·take·account·of·the·new·business·
we·acquired·in·Brussels.·I·enclose·the·current·figures·for·your·reference.·Could·you·
send·me·an·updated·report·as·soon·as·possible·so·that·I·can·forward·it·to·George.¶
¶
▪ Sincerely,¶

▪ ¶
▪ ¶
Patricia·Fellows¶
▪ Enclosures:·1¶
```

To see how the envelope and letter will appear when printed either the Print Preview or Page Layout View options may be taken.

If you want to change any of the formatting in the letter you can do so in just the same way you would had you created the document from scratch. Once you finish using the wizard the document is the same as any other.

Note: *If you plan to print the above exercise, remember that the envelope is on the first page and will be printed first. Ensure an envelope is in the manual feeder of your printer before printing.*

Exercise

1	Use the Fax Wizard to produce a fax using the following information:
2	Fax to:**Global Products Ltd, PO Box 100, Gloucester, G1 4BA** Attn: **Mrs D Gregson, Fax number 0435 678908** From: **Mrs F Hill, Shanghai Lace Industries, Beaverbrook Road**, **Bournemouth, B21 3FG, Fax number 0978 56789**
3	**Further to our telephone conversation this morning, I would like to confirm my order of 14 dozen pearly buttons, reference PB456567.**

Templates

Whilst wizards provide a useful way of creating a customised document it is not always appropriate to follow a step by step series of instructions, or there might not be a wizard for the type of document you want to create. An alternative approach is to use a template.

Word supplies the following template files which are stored on the Template sub-directory of the Winword directory:

Brochur1	Directr1
Faxcovr1	Faxcovr2
Invoice	Letter1

Letter2	Letter3
Manual1	Manuscr1
Manuscr3	Memo1
Memo2	Memo3
Normal	Present1
Presrel1	Presrel2
Presrel3	Purchord
Report1	Report2
Report3	Resume1
Resume2	Resume4
Thesis1	Weektime

To see what any one of these files does select *File | New* to list the templates and then click on a filename. The description box at the bottom of the dialogue box will briefly describe the function of the template.

Like wizards, templates contain all the document and paragraph formatting as well as boilerplate text which can be amended or customised to suit your specific requirement. However a template does not ask you questions like a wizard does, but simply loads a predefined 'template' from which to build a document.

As you can see from the above list, Word supplies a number of templates for business documents including letters, faxes and memos. However, it is likely that these will not exactly suit your requirements and so you can create your own template from which to base future documents. You can either amend an existing template or you can create a new template from an existing document.

Creating a New Template from an Existing One

A customised press release template will be created based on the Word template PRESREL2.

1   Select *File | Open*

2   Select *Document Templates* in the *List Files Of Type* box

3   Change the directory to C:\WINWORD\TEMPLATE

4   Select PRESREL2 and click *OK*

Figure 8.6 shows how the template originally appears. The template includes a date which is currently incorrect. This is a *field code* and will be automatically updated to the current date when the template is used.

Tip: *To see if text is a field code highlight it and it will appear shadowed.*

*Figure 8.6.
PRESREL2.DOT
template.*

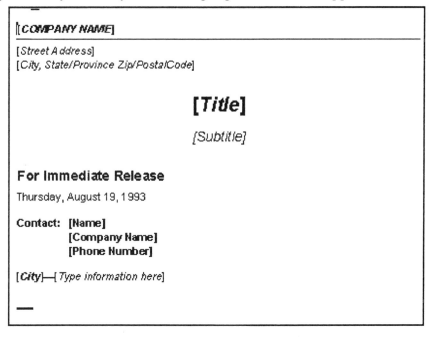

5   Select the first paragraph at the top of the document by triple clicking on the text and then type **BIGJACK PROMOTIONS LTD.**

6   Select the paragraph on the next line and type **3 Galleon Street, Portsmouth, Hants, PO87 5HG.**

7   The remaining information will be filled in when you use the template.

8   To save the file as a new template select *File | Save As.*

   Note: *Be careful not to use the Save command as this will save your changes to the PRESREL2.DOT file.*

9   Type in a new name - **JACK_PR** and click OK

10 Select *File | Close.*

   If you want to store a template in a directory other than \WINWORD\TEMPLATE you must select *Tools | Options*, then click on the *File Locations* tab. Figure 8.7 shows this dialogue box.

*Figure 8.7.
File Locations
Dialogue Box.*

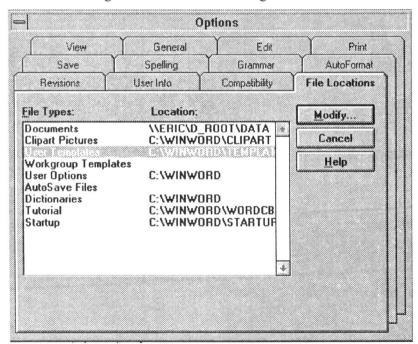

The *User Templates* location can be changed to a directory or your choice. However, if you make this change Word will always look at that directory until the *File Location* is changed again.

Using the Template

The press release template can now be used as the basis for a document.

1   Select *File | New*.

2   From the list of files in the *Template* list select JACK_PR by double-clicking on the name.

Note: *If you want to use the Normal template for a new document you can click on the New button on the Standard toolbar, but if you intend using a different template you must select New from the File menu.*

A new document window is opened with your customised template. Notice that the date is displaying today's date (providing the system date on your computer is correct!).

As you have to highlight existing text to replace it with your own it is advisable to show paragraph marks, so click on the paragraph mark button on the Formatting toolbar if they are not already displayed.

3   Select the word "**[Title]**" - (this one word is a paragraph so if you triple click you will be sure to select the brackets as well) - and type "**CHINESE NEW YEAR**"

4   Select "**[Subtitle]**" on the next line and type **"Dragon Boat Races"**

5   In the area reserved for "**Contact**" type:

Dan Gregson
Daily Dispatch
0345 54321

6   Fill out the rest of the press release with the following text:-

Portsmouth - Tough competition will be out in force again this year when the Portsmouth Dragons take on the Plymouth Devils at the Chinese New Year celebrations in the Harbour.

7   Save the document either by selecting *File | Save* by clicking on the *Save* button on the Standard toolbar, ensure you are in the correct directory and type in a filename - **DRAGONS**. Click *OK* or press ENTER to complete the save.

Note: *The Template file JACK_PR has not been changed and remains on the TEMPLATE directory.*

Exercise

1   Use the Memo1 template as the basis for a new template. The following information about your company must added.

      Hills Laboratories, Cheddar Trading Estate, Cheltenham, Glos, GF34 6PL. Telephone number 0876 34587, Fax number 0876 34588

2   Centre the words "Fax Cover Sheet" and remove the From reference to Company Name

3   Save the template as HILLFAX

4   Create a Fax document using the HILLFAX template with the following information:

      To: Jim Clark at Jennings Test Tubes, Telephone 0987 12345, Fax 0987 23456.

      From: Virginia Wright

      Re: My Order

      This is to confirm my order for two dozen size 2 test tubes for immediate delivery.

Summary

This chapter has provided you with ways to quickly prepare document formats that specifically meet your needs. Wizards prompt you through the process, whilst templates form the fully formatted boilerplate for a document.

Skilful use of the wizards and templates provided by Word will enable you to produce documents that satisfy a wide range of common business tasks.

Self Test

1 What file extension is given by Word to a wizard file?

2 Which view mode should you be in when using a wizard?

3 What does a small square to the left of a paragraph mean?

4 What is the main difference between a wizard and a template?

5 What file extension is given by Word to a template file?

6 Where are template files normally found?

7 When you have customised a template what save command must you use and why?

8 How can you change the location of a template file?

9 How can you obtain a description of a template?

10 What template will be used if you start a new document by clicking on the *New* button on the Standard toolbar?

NINE
Columns, Sections and Tables

Key Learning Points In This Chapter

- Creating documents with multiple columns

- Dividing a document into sections

- Creating and modifying tables

Introduction

Word allows you to format text into two or more *snaking* columns. This means that the text flows from the bottom of one column to the top of the next. Columns can be applied to an entire document or to a *section* of a document.

If you change the page layout one or more times in a document Word controls this through the use of *section breaks* and you will learn how to work with these in this Chapter.

As tables are a form of working with columns of information the creation and modification of tables is also covered here.

Working with Columns

The same document that was used in Chapter Five, PROOF_A is used for the exercises in this chapter. Ensure it is saved in the STEPWORD directory in a fully corrected form with the name COLUMN_A.

1 Open the file COLUMN_A.

2 Select *File | Save As*.

3 Enter the name **COLUMN_1**.

4 Click *OK*.

The *Column* button on the Standard toolbar can be used to create up to five columns in a document or to change the number of existing columns. Word automatically breaks each column at the bottom of a page and moves the remaining text to the top of the next column. However, you can insert your own column breaks if necessary.

1 Click the *Columns* button on the Standard toolbar.

2 Drag to the right to select two columns.

When you release the mouse button, two equal sized columns are created within the current margins of your document. If you are in Normal View you will not be able to see the right hand column.

3   Click on the *Page Layout View* button.

Figure 9.1 shows the screen in Page Layout View.

Figure 9.1.
Document with
two columns.

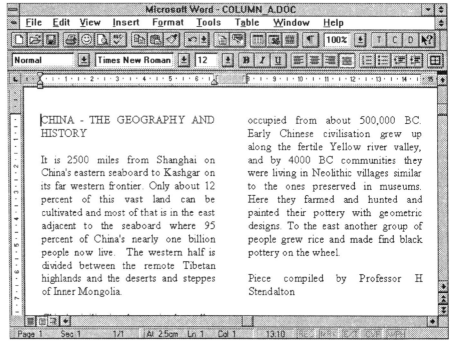

If you look at the bottom of the left-hand column you will see that a paragraph is split across two columns. To force this paragraph onto the second column you can insert a column break.

Place the insertion point at the beginning of the paragraph that starts 'Remains of early man ...'

1   Select *Insert | Break*

2   Click on *Column Break*

3   Click *OK*

There is a **Columns** option on the **Format** menu which includes special formatting options for multiple columns. Figure 9.2 shows the Columns dialogue box.

Exercise

1 Re-open the COLUMN_A file and save as COLUMN_2.

2 Format the document into three columns and place column breaks where necessary so that paragraphs are not split across two columns.

Figure 9.2.
Columns
dialogue box.

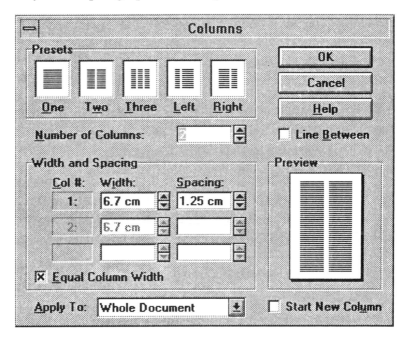

As you can see from Figure 9.2 Word supplies five preset column options and instead of using the *Columns* button on the Formatting toolbar to create the columns you can use this dialogue box to specify one of the preset options.

You can adjust the width of each column, making columns of unequal width if necessary as well as change the spacing between columns. You can also, through this dialogue box, draw a line between columns. To do this,

1 Select *Format* | *Columns*

2 Check the *Line Between* box

3   Click *OK*

4   Save the file before continuing by clicking on the *Save* button.

Section Breaks

Multiple columns are especially useful when you are preparing documents such as a newsletter or brochure. However you will probably not want all the document to be formatted with the same number of columns. Word allows you to have different page layout specifications within a single document through the use of *section breaks*.

Whilst working with section breaks it is advisable to switch to Normal View as you will then see a double dotted line across the screen where you insert section breaks.

In your document COLUMN_1 the title of the article will be a one column section in order that it can be centred across the width of the page. The next paragraph is to be across two columns. A sub-heading will be inserted before the remainder of the article which will then be formatted with three columns.

1   Re-open the file COLUMN_A

2   Select *File | Save As* and enter a new filename of **COLUMN_2**

3   Increase the font size of the title to 14 point using the *Font Size* box on the Formatting Toolbar.

4   Click the *Centre* button on the Formatting toolbar.

5   Click the *Bold* button on the Formatting toolbar.

6   Place the insertion point before the word 'It' at the beginning of the document.

7   Select *Insert | Break*

8   Click the *Continuous* option button in the Section Breaks part of the dialogue box so that the new section will follow directly after the title.

9 Click *OK*

10 Position the insertion point before 'China's civilisation.....'.

11 Type China's Growing Civilisation and press ENTER twice.

12 Select the new heading

13 Click the *Centre* button on the Formatting toolbar.

14 Click the *Bold* button on the Formatting toolbar.

15 Position the insertion point at the end of the first paragraph after the words 'Inner Mongolia'.

16 Select *Insert | Break*

17 Click the *Continuous* option button in the Section Breaks part of the dialogue box.

18 Position the insertion point after the sub-heading and before the first word of the next paragraph ('China's...)

19 Select *Insert | Break*

20 Click the *Continuous* option button in the Section Breaks part of the dialogue box.

21 You now have four sections in the document. If you scroll through the document from the top you will see the section reference at the bottom of the screen change as you move from section to section.

22 The title will remain a single column section

23 Position the insertion point somewhere in the second section

24 Click on the *Columns* button and highlight two columns.

25 The sub-heading will remain a single column section

26 Position the insertion point somewhere in the fourth section

27   Click on the *Columns* button and highlight three columns.

The *column balance* of the last section is not good as the text will flow to the bottom of the page before moving to the next column. To overcome this another section must be inserted at the end of the text which will cause the three columns in the last section to be of equal length.

28   Position the insertion point at the end of the text after 'Standalone.

29   Select *Insert | Break*

30   Click the *Continuous* option button in the Section Breaks part of the dialogue box.

Figure 9.3 shows how the document will now appear.

If you want to change the margins or other page layout features of a particular section you can do this through the *File | Page Setup* menu. In the *Apply To* box, ensure that '*This Section*' is displayed.

Note: *"This Section" will only be an option if your document has multiple sections.*

Exercise

1   Re-open the COLUMN_A file.

2   Centre the title across a single column.

3   Format the body of the text into three columns with vertical lines between them.

4   Centre the last sentence beginning 'Piece compiled ....' across a single column.

Figure 9.3.
Fully formatted
document.

CHINA - THE GEOGRAPHY AND HISTORY

It is 2500 miles from Shanghai on China's eastern seaboard to Kashgar on its far western frontier. Only about 12 percent of this vast land can be cultivated and most of that is in the east adjacent to the seaboard where 95 percent of China's nearly one billion people now live. The western half is divided between the remote Tibetan highlands and the deserts and steppes of Inner Mongolia.

China's Growing Civilisation

China's civilisation began in the valley of the Yellow River, the northernmost of her three great eastward flowing rivers. The Yangtze River, which meats the see near Shanghai, divides south China form the North China Plain. In the mountainous south the West River draws on many tributaries in its path to the sea near Canton. In the north the main crops are millet, maize and wheat. The great rice growing and silk producing areas lie in the Yangtze Valley and the south, whose mountain slopes also produce the teas for which China is famous.

Over most of China a standard form of Chinese derived from Northern Mandarin is now spoken. In the southern provinces the people also maintain their own distinctive dialects, such as Cantonese, with a pronunciation so different and a tonal pattern so complex that they are unintelligible to their compatriots in the north. The south-western provinces are the home of numerous minority peoples and all maintain their own distinctive ways of life.

Remains of early man in China going back to 700,000 BC have been found to the south of Peking, where Peking Man was discovered, and which was occupied from about 500,000 BC. Early Chinese civilisation grew up along the fertile Yellow river valley, and by 4000 BC communities they were living in Neolithic villages similar to the ones preserved in museums. Here they farmed and hunted and painted their pottery with geometric designs. To the east another group of people grew rice and made find black pottery on the wheel.

Piece compiled by Professor H Stendalton

Tables

A table in Word may be defined as a series of rows and columns forming a grid of boxes which are referred to as *cells*. Any cell in a table may contain text or graphics. Text wraps around within a cell in the same way that it wraps around within the margins of a page.

Creating a Table

When a table is inserted each cell is outlined with dotted gridlines and every cell is ended with an *end-of-cell* mark. Neither the gridlines or the end-of-cell marks are printed.

1   Create the file called SALES_A in Appendix B.

2   Select *File | Save As* and save the file as SALES_1.

A table showing the departmental sales figures is to be inserted at the end of the file.

3   Position the insertion point at the end of the file by pressing CRTL+END.

4   Click the *Insert Table* button 🖽 on the Formatting toolbar to display the grid.

5   Highlight three rows and four columns.

When you release the mouse button an empty table with the specified number of rows and columns is inserted into your document, as shown in Figure 9.4.

Figure 9.4. Empty table inserted into document.

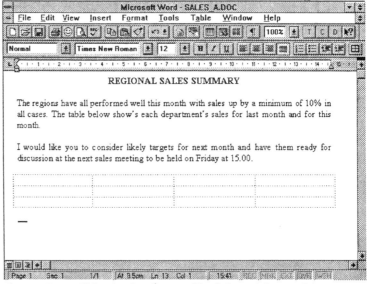

The insertion point will be in the first cell of the table awaiting text entry.

1   Type: **Month**

2   Press   TAB   to   move   to   the   next   cell.

3   Type: **Kent**

4   Press TAB to move to the next cell.

5   Type: **Surrey**

6   Press TAB to move to the next cell.

7   Type: **London**

8   Press TAB to move to the next cell.

        The insertion point moves to the first cell of the next row.

9   Complete the other two rows of the table with the following information.

June	**350**	**410**	**500**
July	**400**	**475**	**580**

        Figure 9.5 shows the completed table.

Figure 9.5.
Completed table.

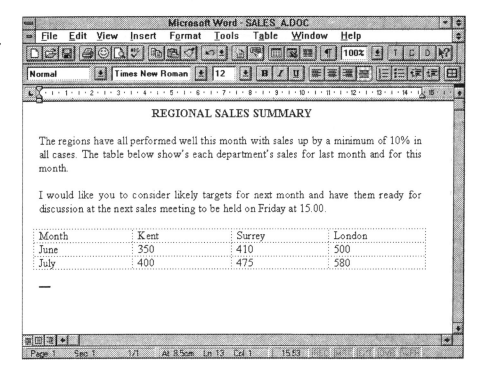

Changing Column Widths

You can adjust the width of the columns using the ruler.

1   Select *View | Ruler* if the ruler is not currently displayed.

2   Click in the first cell of the table containing the word 'Month' which will
display the table column markers on the ruler as shown in Figure 9.6.

*Figure 9.6.
Table column
markers.*

3   Click on the first column marker and drag it to the left to reduce the width of
the column.

4   Repeat the above procedure for the remaining columns.

Instead of manually adjusting the column widths, Word can establish a *best
fit*. This will format each column width to be as wide as the text in the longest
cell in a column without the text wrapping onto two lines.

1   With the insertion point somewhere on the table, highlight the entire table
with *Table | Select Table.*

2   Select *Table | Cell Height And Width*.

3   Click the *AutoFit* button.

Inserting and Deleting Rows and Columns

Rows and columns can be inserted either through the Table menu or by using
the *Table* button on the Standard toolbar. Similarly rows and columns can be
deleted through the Table menu, or the *Cut* button on the Standard toolbar
may be used.

Insert a Row

To insert a row between the titles and the data for June on the table in the
SALES_A document the row below to new row must first be selected:

1　　Click to the left of the second row of the table to select the entire row. (This is much the same as selecting a paragraph).

　　　　Make sure that the entire row is selected and not just the first cell, as a cell can also be selected by clicking on it.

2　　Click the *Table* button on the Standard toolbar.

　　　　Note: *The name and the function of the Table button changes if rows, columns or cells are selected. If you move the pointer to the Table button the prompt box will now read 'Insert Rows' whereas it previously read 'Insert Table'.*

3　　To deselect the rows, click anywhere outside the table.

4　　Place the insertion point on the first cell of the new row and type in the following information, pressing the TAB key to move from cell to cell.

MAY　　300　400　450

　　　　Note: *To insert an additional row at the bottom of a table, place the insertion point in the bottom right most cell and press TAB. A new row is inserted with the same formatting as the one above.*

Insert a Column

The process for selecting a column is similar to that of inserting a row. A new column will be inserted to the right of the Months.

1　　Position the pointer at the top of the second column.

2　　Click when the pointer changes to a down arrow which will select the entire column.

3　　Click the *Table* button, which now has the function of Insert Column.

4　　Enter the following information into the new column, pressing the DOWN ARROW key to move from cell to cell.

　　　　Sussex
　　　　150

200
300

If you need to insert a column to the right side of a table you must select the *end-of-row mark* in the same way that you would select a column. Make sure you are showing markers before attempting to do this. Figure 9.7 shows the table with the additional row and column.

Figure 9.7.
Table with
additional row
and column.

Month	Sussex	Kent	Surrey	London	
May	150	300	400	450	
June	200	350	410	500	
July	300	400	475	580	

Deleting Rows and Columns

To delete the last column of the table:

1   Select the column.

2   Click the *Cut* button on the Standard toolbar.

Rows are deleted in the same way.

Tip: *If you delete a column or row by mistake you can get it back by pressing* CTRL+Z *or by clicking on the Undo button on the Standard toolbar.*

Borders and Shading

Although table gridlines are displayed on the screen, they are not printed. The appearance of a table can be greatly enhanced by adding borders and shading key cells. The *Table* | *AutoFormat* command provides a number of different formatting options that allow you to quickly format a table.

1   Ensure the insertion point is somewhere in the table.

2   Select *Table* | *AutoFormat*

3 Click on the *Classic 1* format option. Figure 9.8 shows the preview of this format option in the dialogue box.

Figure 9.8.
Table AutoFormat
dialogue box.

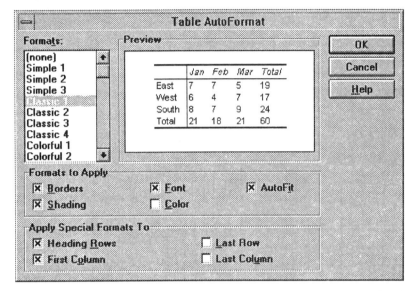

4 Click *OK* to return to the document and have the formatting applied to the table.

Formatting Table Text

Text in the cells of a table can be formatted like any other text in a document. The *Bold*, *Italic* and *Underline* buttons can be used to format one, several or all the cells. In addition cells can be merged in order that text can be spread across a table as opposed to it wrapping around in a single cell.

To put a title into the table:

1 Insert a row by selecting the top row and clicking on the *Table* button.

2 Select the new first row by clicking to the left of the row.

3 Select *Table | Merge Cells*

4 Type: REGIONAL MONTHLY SALES REPORT

The merged cell takes on the formatting of the first cell and thus the text is in italics. In addition there is a right border on this cell which was originally on the first cell. This border is not required with the AutoFormat option being used.

5   Select the merged cell by clicking to the left of it.

6   Click on the *Borders* button on the Formatting toolbar and click the Right Border button to cancel the border.

7   Click the *Bold* button on the Formatting toolbar.

As a final step in the creation of this table, the overall appearance would be improved if the table were centred between the document margins.

1   Select the entire table with *Table | Select Table*.

2   Select *Table | Cell Height and Width.*

3   Select the *Row* tab.

4   Click on the *Center* button in the *Alignment* section.

5   Click *OK* to return to the document and have the table centred.

Exercise

1   Using the Table features create a table that looks like the one shown here.

Duty Roster for Summer 1994				
	May	**June**	**July**	**August**
John	**ON**	**OFF**	**ON**	**OFF**
Simon	**OFF**	**ON**	**ON**	**OFF**
Juliette	**ON**	**ON**	**OFF**	**ON**

Summary

Being able to format documents with multiple columns can add considerable interest to many applications such as newsletters, company brochures, etc., and this chapter has shown you how easy it is to begin working in this way with Word. Furthermore the ease with which tables can be created and formatted makes the preparation of marketing and financial reports a routine task, as opposed to a potentially time consuming and arduous operation.

Self Test

1   How do you format an existing document to be across three columns?

2   What must you do if you want the document title to be centred between the document margins?

3   How do you draw a vertical line between two columns?

4   What command is required to change the formatting of a paragraph to two columns in an otherwise one column document?

5   How do you ensure that columns are balanced?

6   How can you change the margins for a particular section?

7   On which toolbar is the Table button?

8   How do you move across a row from cell to cell when entering text?

9   How do you insert an additional row at the bottom of a table?

10   How do you centre a table between the document margins?

TEN
Graphics and Data Transfer

Key Learning Points in This Chapter

- Importing graphs and pictures
- Linking to other files
- Transferring data with the Clipboard
- Using Dynamic Data Exchange to link with other applications
- Working with Object Linking & Embedding

Introduction

Among the more powerful features of Word is the ability to incorporate information from other Windows applications within your documents. This makes it easy to produce sophisticated and informative reports, proposals, newsletters etc. In fact you are only really limited by your imagination and the versatility of the other applications that you have.

There are a number of different ways to transfer information into Word. Some are *static*, which means that once combined the data only changes if you edit it within Word, whilst other techniques are *dynamic*, meaning that the copy of the data that you have in Word is *linked* to the original application and can be updated if the original information is changed.

The techniques examined in this chapter comprise a mixture of static and dynamic methods. Furthermore they are complementary, which means you might use a combination of static and dynamic techniques when transferring data.

Inserting From Disk

You can take an existing data file from the disk and *insert* it into your document. The file could be produced by a spreadsheet, word processor, database or graphics program, and once inserted it may be edited with the features provided by Word. To insert a file from disk, the Word *Insert* command is used, and you can choose whether the link is dynamic or static.

Clipboard

The clipboard allows you to use the *Copy* and *Paste* options under the *Edit* menu to transfer data from one Windows application to another. It is a static technique, but is very quick and easy to use.

Dynamic Data Exchange (DDE)

DDE is similar to the Clipboard, except that it is dynamic. It may be used to transfer and link spreadsheet figures into your documents, as it allows updates made to the figures to be automatically reflected in Word.

Object Linking and Embedding (OLE)

OLE is the most flexible technique, as it may be either dynamic or static, and may be established through the *Edit* menu or the *Insert* menu options. Word supports the OLE 2 standard, so is able to work with almost every other application that provides OLE features.

Loading Pictures From Disk

One of the easiest ways to incorporate pictures and images is to load an existing picture from the disk. This could have been produced with a drawing program such as Corel DRAW! or Lotus Freelance, or it may be a graph from a spreadsheet such as Lotus 1-2-3.

File Formats

The file formats recognised by Word are dependent upon the installation technique chosen. For example, using the Custom installation method it is possible to choose to omit specific file converters, which would prevent Word from being to load files of that type.

If you had performed a complete installation when initially setting up the software, then Word will recognise eight different file types. The full list of file formats supported is as follows.

DrawPerfect	Micrografx Designer/Draw
Computer Graphics Metafile (CGM)	Encapsulated PostScript (EPS)
Tag Image File Format (TIFF)	Macintosh PICT
PCX	Compuserve GIF

When you attempt to load a file from disk, Word examines it to see if it is one of the recognised formats. If so it will be loaded, otherwise an error message will be displayed.

Loading a Picture

Pictures are loaded into a document through the *Insert | Picture* commands. The dialogue box produced when these commands are selected is shown in Figure 10.1:

*Figure 10.1.
The Insert Picture
dialogue box.*

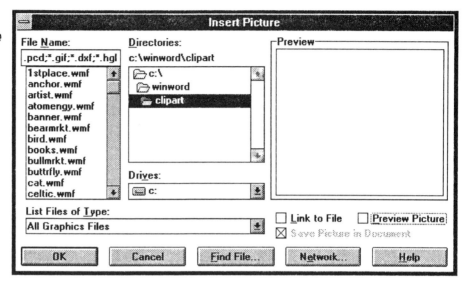

The *List Files of Type* option currently specifies "All Graphics Files". The arrow to the right of the text can be clicked to drop down a list of available graphics file formats, together with their default extensions. If you know that you are looking for a specific file type, such as a Lotus PIC file then the "Lotus 1-2-3 Graphics" option could be selected instead, thus limiting the list of displayed files to those with a PIC extension only.

The *Preview Picture* check box can be selected if you want to see a simplified image of the picture as you highlight its name in the list. This is useful if you know what the picture looks like, but can't quite remember what it was called or where it was stored.

1 Create a new document by clicking the *New* button.

2 Type the following text: **The following logo has been loaded from the disk**.

3 Press ENTER twice, to give two blank paragraphs.

4 Select *Insert | Picture*.

5   Change the directory to C:\WINWORD\CLIPART. If you installed Word into a directory other than C:\WINWORD then you should use this location instead.

6   If no Clipart is available (perhaps because you performed a minimal installation) then change the directory to C:\WINWORD\WORDCBT, which should contain some graphics files.

7   Select one of the WMF files listed and click *OK*.

8   Save the document as PICDEMO1.

Positioning and Sizing Pictures

Having loaded the picture into the document it can be positioned, sized and formatted as required.

Positioning Pictures

Positioning is defined by the margins, indents, spacing and alignment of the paragraph. For example, if you wanted to centre the picture you would use the Centre button on the toolbar.

If you require more controllable positioning for a picture, for example at a specific location on the page, then a *frame* can be used. Frames are boxes that are inserted into the document using **Insert | Frame**, and can hold any combination of text, graphics, tables etc.

Sizing Pictures

Sizing is controlled with the mouse, or through the **Format | Picture** command.

To use the mouse, click on the picture to select it. Once selected it will be shown with 8 *handles* around its perimeter, as shown in Figure 10.2. Clicking and dragging any of these handles allows the picture to be resized. Dragging a corner handle results in the *aspect ratio* (height : width) being maintained, so the picture keeps the original proportions. The handles on the sides allow the picture to be stretched to any aspect ratio, allowing simple special effects to be created.

Figure 10.2.
Picture sizing
handles.

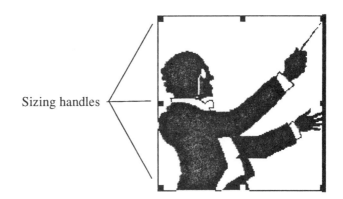

Sizing handles

The *Format | Picture* command produces the dialogue box shown here in Figure 10.3.

Figure 10.3.
Picture
formatting
dialogue box.

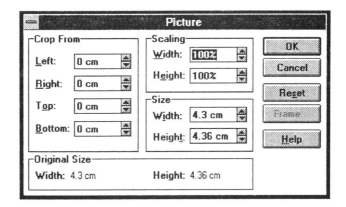

These options allow the height and width to be set, either in measurement units such as centimetres, or as a percentage of the original size. The cropping options allow you to prevent part of the picture from being displayed. For example, if you have a graphic that you want to display, but not show the outermost 1cm all round, setting cropping values of 1cm for Left, Right, Top and Bottom would do this for you.

Setting the cropping values to negative values results in a white space or border being displayed around the outside of the image.

Figure 10.4 shows the conductor image cropped by 1cm at the top and bottom, with no cropping on the left or right.

Figure 10.4.
A cropped
image.

1   Open the PICDEMO1 file, if it's not already opened.

2   Click on the picture to select it.

3   Click the *Right Alignment* button on the toolbar; the picture is positioned on the right of the page.

4   Drag the sizing handle at the bottom right of the picture to make the box about 50% bigger.

Note that when you release the button the picture is enlarged, but still maintains its alignment on the page.

5   Select *Format | Picture*.

6   Click on the *Reset* button; the picture is returned to the original size, but the right alignment is maintained.

Linking a Picture

A picture that is loaded using the previous techniques is a once-only transfer; if the picture file is updated on disk then the image in the document will not change, unless you insert it a second time.

If you do want the image to be updated then you can *link* the picture rather than just load it. This is achieved by choosing the *Link to File* check box from the *Insert | Picture* dialogue box, as highlighted in Figure 10.5.

Figure 10.5.
Linking a picture.

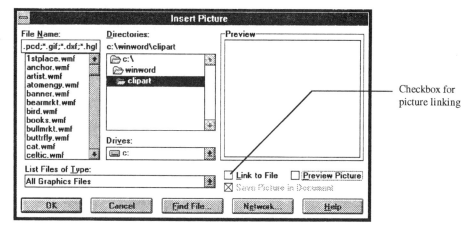

Having linked the picture in this way it can be managed through the *Edit |*
Links command. This provides options for updating, cancelling and changing
the behaviour of the link.

1 Switch to *Program Manager* and run the *Paintbrush* application from the
accessories group (if you have another drawing program with which you
are familiar then you may want to use this instead).

2 Create a simple image using Paintbrush (it needn't represent anything, just
a couple of curved or straight lines will do).

3 Save the file to the disk as LINKDIAG.

4 Close Paintbrush and switch back to Word.

5 Create a new document.

6 Select *Insert | Picture* to display the dialogue box.

7 Click on the *Link to File* option to place a checkmark in the box, then find
the file that you created (LINKDIAG.BMP) and double-click to load it
into Word.

8 Save the document as PICDEMO2.

9   Switch back to Program Manager, run Paintbrush again, and load the LINKDIAG.BMP file.

10   Make a change to the image by adding or removing some lines or circles, then save the file to the disk.

11   Close Paintbrush and return to Word.

12   Word has NOT, as you might have expected, updated the picture. Instead the original image is still displayed.

13   In order to update it, select the image in the document and select *Edit | Links*.

14   Click on the *Update Now* button in the dialogue box, then select Close.

Further options are available through the Links dialogue box. These allow the link to be changed from a manual link, which requires updating, to an automatic link which ensures the loaded image is always the same as the image on the disk. You can also break the link, lock the link and change the source of the link. These options are discussed fully in the help system and the Word documentation.

Exercise

1   Insert the picture called CAT.WMF into the ALICE_A.DOC file. This image can be found in the CLIPART directory, and should be positioned between the first and second paragraphs of the document. Save the file as ALICE_P1.DOC.

2   Open ALICE_A again. Format the document into two columns, and insert the CAT.WMF file at the end of the text and balance the columns so that the bottom of the picture lines up with the bottom of the first column of text.

The Clipboard

The Clipboard is used during the *Cut*, *Copy* and *Paste* operations discussed in Chapter Three. Put simply, the Clipboard is a general-purpose storage area, which can hold any type and amount of information from your application. Once information is placed onto the Clipboard, it remains there until you exit Windows, or until something else is placed onto the Clipboard instead.

- Information is transferred *to* the Clipboard using the ***Edit | Cut*** and ***Edit | Copy*** commands. Remember that Cut removes the original information, whereas Copy duplicates it.

- Information is transferred *from* the Clipboard using the ***Edit | Paste*** command. Remember that Paste can be used any number of times as the data stays on the Clipboard until it is replaced.

In addition to working within an application, the Clipboard can be used to transfer information between applications, even applications of different types. For example, it is quite possible to use the Clipboard to transfer a picture from Paintbrush into Word.

Copying an Image Using the Clipboard

1   Switch to Program Manager and start Paintbrush.

2   Create a simple image in Paintbrush.

3   Click on the selection tool at the top right of the Paintbrush toolbar

4   Drag a rectangle around the section of your image that you want to copy.

5   Select ***Edit | Copy*** to copy the image to the Clipboard.

6   Close Paintbrush.

7   Switch back to Word and create a new document.

8   Select ***Edit | Paste*** to transfer the picture into the document.

The selected portion of the image is brought into the document and can be positioned and sized in the same way as a loaded picture.

Dynamic Data Exchange (DDE)

The Clipboard techniques produce a non-changing or *static* copy of the original data within your document. If you want a dynamic copy, that is linked to original data in another application then you need to use a different technique. One of the options for this is to *use Dynamic Data Exchange*, although there are some other methods available as well.

The easiest way to create a DDE link is via the *Edit | Paste Special* command, which produces the dialogue box shown in Figure 10.6. In fact this dialogue box is also used when working with Object Linking and Embedding (OLE) techniques as well which is discussed later in this chapter.

*Figure 10.6.
Paste Special
dialogue box.*

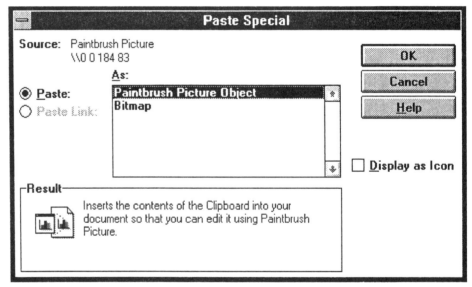

Creating a Link

The creation of a DDE link is very similar to the copy and paste technique used for the Clipboard.

1   Switch to Program Manager and run Paintbrush.

2   Create a simple image and save it to the disk as LINK2.BMP. You *must* save the picture in order for DDE to work.

3 Using the selection tool, highlight an area of your image and copy it to the Clipboard.

4 Without closing Paintbrush, switch to Word and create a new document.

5 Choose *Edit | Paste Special*.

6 Change the type of data to *Bitmap*, then click on the *Paste Link* button.

7 Click on the *OK* button to paste the image and return to the document.

8 Save the document as PICDEMO3.

Updating Linked Data

Having created the link, and changes to the original file will be automatically reflected in the linked copy.

1 Switch to Paintbrush, leaving Word open with your document loaded.

2 Make a change to your image (LINK2.BMP) within the area that you copied to the Clipboard.

3 Switch back to Word and you will see that the change has been automatically made to the copy of the image in your document.

Changing a Link

Having made the change to the original picture, you will have seen that there was a small delay when the image was updated in Word. As you use more and more DDE links within a document you may find that the time taken to update them becomes extended, and could slow the entire system down quite considerably.

Therefore you may choose to change the type of the link from an *Automatic* link to a *Manual* link. As you would expect, the automatic link reflects any changes to the original information immediately, whereas the manual link requires that you choose the *Update Now* button from the Links dialogue box to make the changes appear. This dialogue box is shown in Figure 10.7.

Figure 10.7.
The Links
dialogue box.

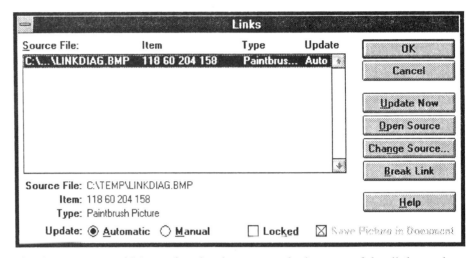

The *Automatic* and *Manual* option buttons at the bottom of the dialogue box define the link type, whilst the buttons to the right are used to manage the link. Note that if there are multiple links within a document it is only the highlighted one that is affected if you change any settings. If more than one link is to be modified then CTRL click each of them before changing the settings, as this allows multiple selections to be made.

1   Choose *Edit | Links* to display the dialogue box.

2   Ensure the link to Paintbrush is selected.

3   Click on the *Manual* option button, then click OK.

4   Switch to Paintbrush, leaving Word open with your document loaded.

5   Make a change to your image (LINK2.BMP) within the area that you copied to the Clipboard.

6   Switch back to Word. You will find that the change you have just made in Paintbrush is not yet reflected in Word.

7   Select *Edit | Links* again and choose the *Update Now* button.

8   The document image is updated to show the recent changes.

Object Linking & Embedding (OLE)

The third data transfer technique is to use Object Linking and Embedding. This is the most flexible technique as it provides a similar set of features to the Clipboard and DDE combined. However, OLE is not as widely supported as the Clipboard or DDE, although all of the Microsoft Office applications (Word, Excel etc.) support OLE fully.

The two main ways to include OLE information in a Word document are through the use of the *Edit | Paste Special* command, and through the *Insert | Object* command.

Having created the object it will look almost the same as if it had been created with the Clipboard or with DDE. It is only when you start to change the data that the differences become apparent.

Pasting an Object

1   Switch to Program Manager and run Paintbrush.

2   Create a simple image. Unlike DDE, there is no need to save the image to the disk.

3   Using the selection tool, highlight an area of your image and copy it.

4   Switch to Word and create a new document.

5   Select *Edit | Paste Special*.

6   Ensure the type is *Paintbrush Picture Object*, then click the *Paste* button.

7   Click on the *OK* button to paste the image and return to the document.

It is also possible to create a linked object, by saving the original file before copying the data, then choosing the *Paste Link* option. This will behave in much the same way as a link created using the DDE techniques discussed previously.

Inserting an Object

Rather than having to manually launch the application supplying the data, this technique allows you to use the features of Word to start the program for you.

1   Within Word close any documents you may have open, then create another new one.

2   Select *Insert | Object*.

3   Scroll down the *Object* list and select *Paintbrush Picture*.

4   Click on *OK* and Word will automatically launch Paintbrush.

5   Draw a simple image.

6   Select *Exit & Return to Document1*.

7   A dialogue box asks whether the image should be updated. Click on *Yes* to ensure that the image is transferred into your document.

8   On returning to Word you will find the image has been inserted into the document. As with any picture it can be positioned and sized as required.

   As you will see, the Object dialogue box lists many different object types, some of which are supplied with Word (such as a *Microsoft Word 6.0 Picture*) whilst others relate to other applications (such as *Paintbrush Picture*).

Editing an Object

An object can be changed or updated very easily. Double clicking the object within the document causes the original (source) application to be executed and the data loaded into it. Having completed the changes the *File | Exit* command will return you to Word.

1   Double-click the insert Paintbrush Picture.

2   Once Paintbrush has loaded, make some changes to the picture.

3   Select *File | Exit & Return to Document1* to return to Word.

Exercise

> **1**   Use the *Insert | Object* command to insert a *Microsoft Word 6.0 Picture* into your document. You will find that this loads a drawing program that allows you to create quite sophisticated and detailed diagrams.
>
> **2**   Experiment with the other object types available. Remember that any object that is prefixed with *Microsoft Word 6.0* is supplied with Word, and so will be referenced in the documentation and will be supported with detailed on-line help.

Summary

The graphics and data transfer features of Word are extremely powerful, and this chapter has only begun to demonstrate what can be achieved through their use.

When working with a suite of Windows applications, such as the Microsoft Office products, these features guarantee that the different programs can efficiently transfer data to one another with a minimum of effort. For example, if you had created a financial plan spreadsheet in Excel, either the Clipboard, DDE or OLE could be used to transfer that information into Word.

When choosing between these techniques remember their key differences. The Clipboard provides a once-only transfer which will not be automatically updated under any circumstances. DDE allows the data to be updated either automatically or manually, but can slow the system down. OLE provides an easy way to edit the information, but does have a tendency to substantially increase the size of the document files, thus consuming more disk space.

Self Test

1   How many graphic file formats can Word recognise?

2   What command is used to insert a picture into a Word document?

3   How can you preview a picture prior to inserting it into a document?

4   Which directory does Word store the provided clipart in?

5   What is the difference between using a corner handle and a side handle
          when resizing a picture?

6   What is the effect of the *Link To File* command?

7   What does DDE stand for and what is the benefit of using this technique?

8   When working with a DDE link, what is the difference between a *manual*
          and an *automatic* link?

9   What does OLE stand for and how does it differ from DDE?

10   How do you edit an image that has been inserted into a document as an
          OLE object?

ELEVEN
Merged Documents

Key Learning Points In This Chapter

- Create a document into which variable information, such as names and addresses, can be placed.
- Create a data file of names and addresses.
- Merge the names and addresses with the main document.

Introduction

As the term implies, a merged document requires two files - the *main document* and the *data file*.

The main document contains standardised text and graphics that you want to repeat with different variable information inserted into it. In the main document you insert special *merge fields* which indicate to Word where the variable information is to appear. When you merge the data file and the main document, Word inserts the appropriate information from the data file into the merge fields of the main document.

The creation of the main document and the merging of that document with a data file is controlled by the *Mail Merge Helper* supplied by Word to guide you through the steps required.

The most common use of merged documents is the creation of standard letters that you want to send to a number of different people and it this application that will be used as the example in this chapter.

Create The Main Document

1   Close any existing documents with *File | Close*

2   Click on the New button to open a new document using the Normal template.

3   Select *Tools | Mail Merge*

    The dialogue box will appear as shown in Figure 11.1.

4   Click the *Create* button which lists the main document options to choose from.

5   Select *Form Letters* which produces the message shown in Figure 11.2.

Figure 11.1.
Mail Merge
dialogue box.

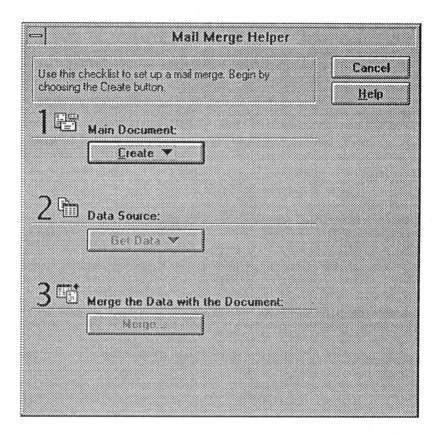

Figure 11.2.
Active window
message.

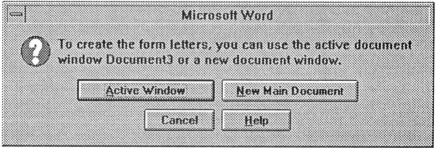

6 Click on the *Active Window* box as you have already opened a new document.

Your main document has now been created and before preparing the standard letter it is necessary to create the data file.

Create The Data File

A data file contains all the text and graphics that will change with each version of the merged document. Each set of related information, such as name, company, address details, is called a *data record* and any single piece of information, such as name, is called a *field*. Therefore a data file consists of a number of data records which in turn consist of a number of fields.

The Mail Merge Helper dialogue box should still be on the screen. If it is not select *Tools | Mail Merge*

1   Select *Create Data Source* which displays the dialogue box shown in Figure 11.3.

Figure 11.3.
Create Data
Source dialogue
box.

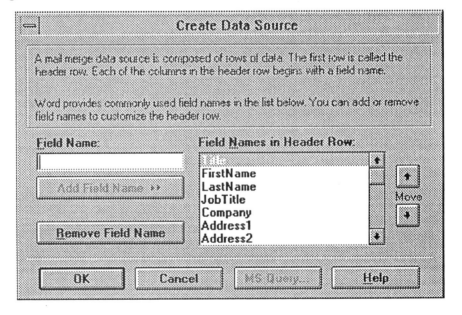

In this dialogue box you can specify the field names to include in the data file. A list of likely fields are suggested which you can use. You can also add your own and you can remove the ones you do not want to use. A field name may consist of up to 40 characters. A name must start with a letter, and subsequent characters must be letters, numbers, or the underscore (_). No spaces are allowed.

2   Scroll through the *Field Names in Header Row* and select **State**.

3   Click on *Remove Field Name.*

4   Remove the following field names:

Country
HomePhone
WorkPhone

5   Into the *Field Name* box type: **County**.

6   Click on *Add Field Name.*

7   Use the up arrow on the *Move* box to the right of the dialogue box to position the field name County before Postcode.

8   Into the *Field Name* box type: **Results**.

9   Click on *Add Field Name.*

10   Click *OK* and the *Save Data Source* box is displayed.

11   Ensure you are in the STEPWORD directory and type **DATA_1** as the filename.

12   Click *OK*.

A dialogue box is displayed to inform you that the data file has no records in it and gives you the choice of entering data now or returning to the main document.

13   Click the *Edit Data Source* button.

The Data Form dialogue box appears as shown in Figure 11.4.

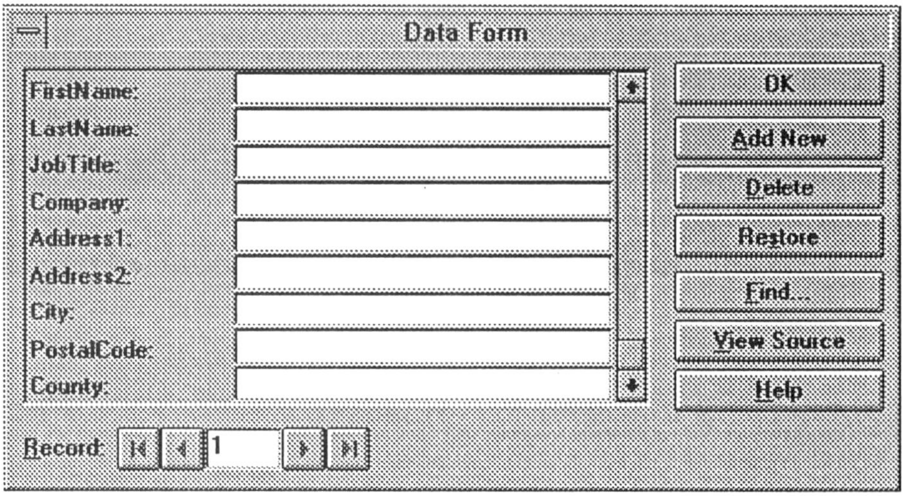

*Figure 11.4.
Data Form
dialogue box.*

Entering Data

You can now enter the details for the first person to whom the letter is to be sent.

1   Type the following information into the form, pressing ENTER at the end of each field.

**Mrs
Diane
King
Marketing Manager
Grosvenor Cutlery
45 Gregson Place
Central Business Park
Gloucester
GLOS
G34 6HP
80%**

2   When you have entered the last field you can either press enter to begin a new record or you can click on *Add New*.

Tip: *If you want to move back to a field in the data form, press* SHIFT+TAB.

3   Add two more data records with the following information. Note that the last record has the second address line blank. Word will skip this line when the data is merged.

Title	**Mr**
FirstName	**Henry**
LastName	**Jinks**
JobTitle	**Marketing Assistant**
Company	**Beds Galore**
Address1	**4 High Street**
Address2	**Little Marsham**
City	**Oxford**
County	**OXON**
PostalCode	**OX3 4PK**
Results	**75%**

Title	**Ms**
FirstName	**Sally**
LastName	**Ellis**
JobTitle	**Director**
Company	**Sally's Curtains**
Address1	**2 Coopers Lane**
Address2	
City	**Redhill**
County	**Surrey**
PostalCode	**RH4 7DF**
Results	**90%**

4   Click OK

You are returned to the main document and the Mail Merge Toolbar is displayed at the top of the screen.

Completing the Main Document

The letter that is to be sent to the addressees in the data file must now be created. References to the field names in the data file will be inserted into the document at the location the variable information is required.

With the insertion point at the beginning of the document insert the current date:

1   Select *Insert |Date And Time*.

2   Click on the second format option.

3   Click *OK*.

4   Select the date and click the *Right Justify* button to position the date on the right side of the page.

5   Press ENTER three times.

The date is inserted into the document as a *field code* and will automatically be updated each time the file is opened.

The first line of the address area is to contain information from the Title, FirstName and LastName fields.

6   On the Mail Merge toolbar, click the *Insert Merge Field* button.

7   A list of the available field names is displayed.

8   Click on the already highlighted Title to insert it into the document.

9   Press SPACEBAR to insert a blank space after the title.

10   Click the *Insert Merge Field* button again.

11   Select *FirstName* and press the SPACEBAR

12   Click the *Insert Merge Field* button and select *LastName*.

Your document will appear as shown in Figure 11.5.

Figure 11.5. Main document with merge field references.

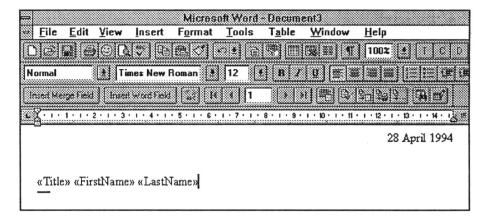

Complete the address as follows:

1   Press ENTER to move to the next line.

2   Click the *Insert Merge Field* button, select *Company* and press ENTER.

3   Click the *Insert Merge Field* button, select *Address1* and press ENTER.

4   Click the *Insert Merge Field* button, select *Address2* and press ENTER.

5   Click the *Insert Merge Field* button, select *City* and press ENTER.

6   Click the *Insert Merge Field* button, select *County* and type a comma and a SPACE.

7   Click the *Insert Merge Field* button, select *PostalCode* and press ENTER.

8   Press ENTER twice and enter the salutation.

9   Type: **Dear** | SPACEBAR .

10 Click the *Insert Merge Field* button, select *Title* and press SPACEBAR.

11 Click the *Insert Merge Field* button, select *LastName* and press ENTER twice.

12 You can now continue to type the body of the letter and you can include merge field names in the letter as well. Use the *Insert Merge Field* button where the fields are indicated below.

Thank you for attending our Marketing skills training course last week. I enclose your certificate and am pleased to tell you that you gained a mark of <<Results>> for the final test. The next course we will be running in the <<City>> area will be in August.

Yours sincerely

Michael Watson

13 Save the file with *File | Save* and enter the name **MAIN_1**

Merging Documents

You are now ready to combine the main document with the data file. Using the buttons on the Mail Merge Toolbar you have three options:

- Use the *Check For Errors* button, ▦ to have Word check that the references in the data file and the main document match correctly and alert you if there are any errors.

- Use the *Merge To Printer* button, ▦ to merge the main document with the data file directly to the printer

- Use the *Merge To New Document* button, ▦ to merge the data file and the main document into a new file that you can read, edit or change before printing at a later stage.

As you may not currently be connected to a printer we will use the third option in this exercise.

1 Click the *Merge To New Document* button.

Each letter is separated with a double dotted line which indicates a section break. Each section is automatically formatted to begin on a new page as shown in Figure 11.6.

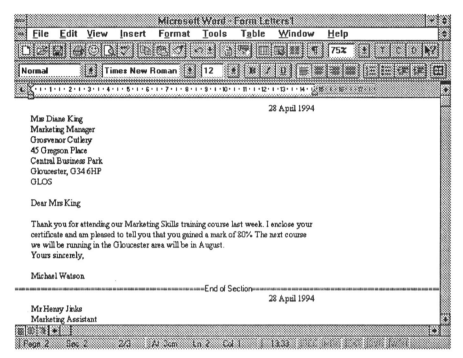

*Figure 11.6.
Completed
Standard letter
with section
break.*

If you scroll through the three letters you will notice that the missing address line on the third letter has been closed up. This file is a normal document file now that can be edited and amended as required. You can then save it and print it in the usual way.

Summary

This chapter has shown you how to merge two documents to produce a standard letter that can be sent to a number of recipients. However, the process of merging a data file with a main document can be used in a wide range of applications and can greatly speed up the production of periodic reports that are based on the same information.

Self Test

1   From which menu will you find the Mail Merge option?

2   What must you create first in the Mail Merge process?

3   What is the difference between a data record and a data field?

4   What are the rules for field names in the Data Source file?

5   How do you change the position of a field in a data record?

6   How can you add a new field into a data record?

7   How can you move back to a field in the data form to make a correction?

8   What button is used to insert a merge field into the main document?

9   What does the Merge to Printer button on the Mail Merge toolbar do?

10   How is each letter separated if a data file is merged to a new document?

TWELVE
Macros

Key Learning Points In This Chapter

- Recording, writing and running macros.

- Customising toolbars.

- Assigning shortcut keys.

Introduction

Macros are among the most powerful features of any application, and have been present in most PC applications since the early commercial software packages became available. Put simply, a macro is a sequence of commands or keystrokes that is stored within the program in a form that can quickly be recalled and executed. This means that they can be used to speed up repetitive tasks, to automate complex routines and to simplify the process of using the program.

Each macro language tends to use a completely different set of commands. Some, such as the early spreadsheets, are little more than sets of keystrokes, whilst the more modern software usually implements macros using English-like commands and statements. Word falls into the latter category, making the macros relatively easy to read and understand. This obviously helps somewhat when it comes to working with macros, although as you will see it is not strictly necessary to understand these commands in order to make use of simple macros.

What are Macros Used For?

As noted previously, macros can be used for many different tasks including speeding up and automating repetitive procedures. Macros can also be used to automate an entire process, allowing you to write a complete document production and management system.

For example, a macro-driven system could be written to ask the user what type of document they wanted to create, and then produce the outline of the document including company logos, mottoes, addresses, registration details etc., according to a predefined style. The user could then fill in the relevant information, such as the main text of the letter, report or proposal, after which the macro could ensure that it was printed on the correct printer, with the appropriate paper (headed, continuation, plain) and could even automatically produce envelopes or mailing labels as necessary.

Where are Macros Stored?

Word stores the macros that are created in templates, either in a specifically named template or in the NORMAL.DOT template. When you create the macro you need to choose where it will be stored, as this will have a bearing on when it can be used.

Template Macros

Macros stored in named templates can only be used within documents based on those named templates. Therefore this approach may not be suitable for macros that you will use on a day-to-day basis as you are likely to be working with several different templates.

Global Macros

Macros stored in NORMAL.DOT are globally available, and can be called and accessed from within any document. Therefore this approach is preferred for general purpose macros, such as those you might use to speed up tasks such as formatting, working with graphics, and printing.

However, if too many macros are stored in NORMAL.DOT then you may become confused as to exactly which ones you should be working with at any time. As you will see, the use of descriptive macro names helps to solve this problem.

How are Macros Created?

Two approaches can be used for creating macros; recording or writing. These techniques are complimentary, with recorded macros often being used as the basis for a complete written macro.

Recording Macros

Recording a macro to automate something is as easy as going through that process manually. The only difference is that prior to starting the procedure you switch on the macro recorder. From that point on, every keystroke or command that you issue will be recorded by the system until you turn the macro recorder off again.

The main macro dialogue box is accessed by choosing the Tools, Macro menu commands, which produces the box shown in Figure 12.1:

Figure 12.1.
The Macro
dialogue box.

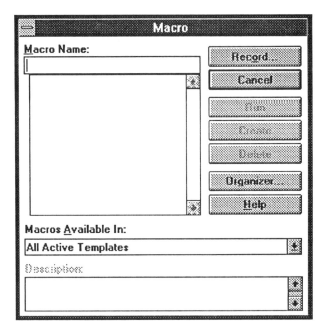

From here, the *Record* button can be clicked to produce the dialogue box shown in Figure 12.2:

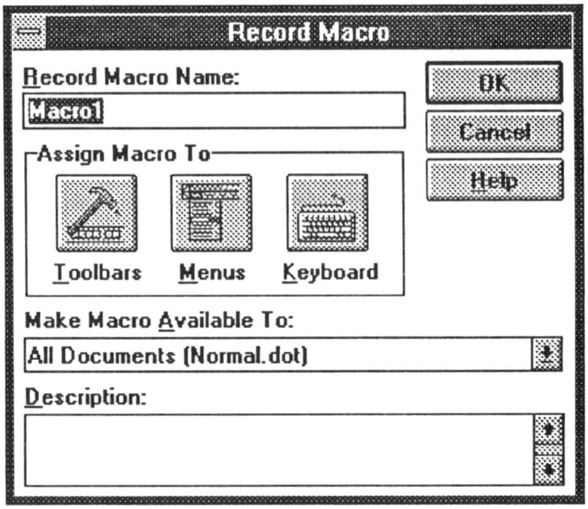

Figure 12.2.
The Record
Macro dialogue
box.

This dialogue box allows the macro's details to be defined, including what it will be called, how it should be activated and where it will be stored. An optional description can also be added to allow you to see exactly what the macro does when you work with it at a later stage. All of these details can be modified subsequently, although it is best to get them correct from the start.

After clicking the *OK* button, the Record Macro dialogue box is removed from the screen and the Macro Record toolbar appears in its place. Also the REC indicator on the status bar at the bottom of the screen is highlighted to show that you are in record mode. These features are shown in Figure 12.3:

Figure 12.3. Macro Recording toolbar and indicator.

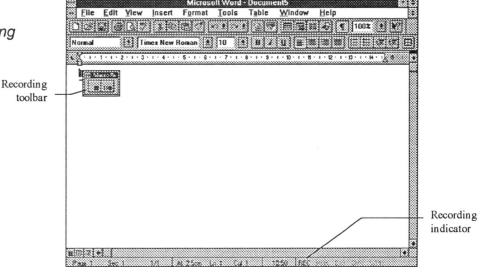

From this point on, everything you do within Word is recorded into the macro. This includes mouse movements and actions, menu selections as well as typing and keyboard shortcuts that are used. The recording is ended either by clicking the *Stop* button on the Macro Record toolbar, or by selecting *Stop Recording* from the main Macro dialogue box. Figure 12.4 shows the Macro Record toolbar as it is displayed when recording begins.

Figure 12.4. Macro Record toolbar.

Recording a Simple Macro

The following will produce a macro that formats the sentence containing the insertion point to bold, italic, and places quotation marks around it.

1   Open the file ALICE_A.DOC if not.

2   Click on the first paragraph of text to position the insertion point.

3   Access the Macro dialogue box by selecting *Tools | Macro.*

4   Click on the *Record* button.

5   Type the name of the macro as **QuotesBoldItalPara.**

6   Type a description for the macro - **This macro emboldens, italicises and quotes the current sentence.**

7   Click the *OK* button to start recording.

8   The procedure to record is quite straightforward.

•   Press F8 three times to highlight the current sentence, then press ESC to exit Extend mode. Alternatively press and hold CTRL then click the sentence to highlight it.

•   Press CTRL+B and CTRL+I to embolden and italicise the text.

•   Press the left arrow once to go to the start of the highlighted area, and enter a quote character – ".

•   Press F8 three times again, followed by ESC and the right arrow key to move to the end of the sentence.

•   Enter a second quote character – " – at the end of the sentence.

9   Stop the macro recorder by clicking the Stop button on the Macro Record toolbar [■].

The macro has now been recorded and stored in the global template (NORMAL.DOT).

Writing Macros

Whilst the recording technique can be used for the majority of "speed-up" type macros, it does not lend itself well to certain tasks, and provides no way at all to access features such as custom dialogue boxes and the structured macro commands that allow looping and conditional macros to be produced.

Thus in order to make the most of the macro language, it will be necessary to write certain macros without the assistance of the recorder. This is done by selecting *Tools | Macro* to access the macro dialogue box, entering a name for the macro and choosing the *Create* button. Word then produces an almost blank macro document, containing only the "**Sub MAIN**" and "**End Sub**" statements to signify the start and end of the macro code. For example, Figure 12.5 shows the window produced when creating a macro called DisplayDialogue.

Figure 12.5.
Writing a macro.

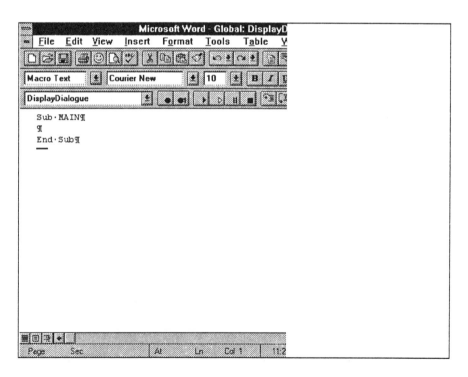

All of the code for the macro is placed between these two statements.

Editing A Macro

As an example of what macro code actually looks like, examine the previously recorded macro (QuotesBoldItalPara):

1   Select *Tools* | *Macro* to access the macro dialogue box

2   Click on the name of the macro in the list

3   Select the *Edit* button

4   The macro text is then displayed in its own document window, which can be closed, minimised, maximised or restored in the same way as any other document window. Notice that the title bar shows the name of the macro as "Global: QuotesBoldItalPara".

5   Close the window to return to your document

Exercise

1   Record a macro, called "DoubleIndent" that indents both the right and left indent markers for the current paragraph by 2cm.

2   Examine the macro code that you have recorded using the *Edit* button from the Macro dialogue box, and obtain a hard copy of the macro if you have a printer.

3   Use the *Create* button of the Macro dialogue box to write a macro that outdents the left and right indents by 2cm each.

Note: *As we haven't yet seen how to run a macro you will not be able to test your code. However, we will address this topic next.*

Running Macros

Macros can be executed in a number of different ways, and as with most Windows features there are techniques that allow you to use menus, buttons or keyboard shortcuts.

Using the Menus

The menu options provide one of the most straightforward ways to run a macro. By selecting *Tools | Macro* the now familiar Macro dialogue box is produced. If a macro name is double-clicked, or if it is highlighted and the *Run* button chosen, then the macro code is executed immediately. Obviously you need to ensure that you have positioned the insertion point appropriately for the macro you want to run.

1   Click in a paragraph of text to position the insertion point. Remember that this macro is designed to highlight a sentence, so choose an appropriate one.

2   Select *Tools | Macro* to display the Macro dialogue box.

3   Either double-click the *QuotesBoldItalPara* macro name, or single click it and then click the *Run* button.

4   The macro should play back the precise sequence of commands that you issued when you recorded it.

If for some reason it doesn't work then try recording the same process again.

Using Toolbars

Macros such as the ones that you have created are likely to be used many times over, and are designed to speed up these repetitive tasks. Therefore it would be preferable to execute the macros with fewer mouse clicks than are required to run the macro using the above technique, and one way to do this is to assign the macro to a button on the toolbar.

This can be achieved through the *Tools | Customise* menu commands, which produces the dialogue box shown in Figure 12.6

Figure 12.6.
The Customise
dialogue box.

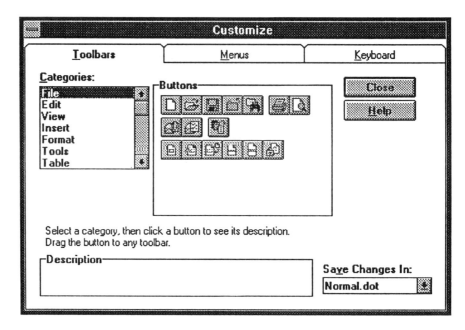

These options allow toolbars, menu options or keyboard shortcuts to be customised as required, including for use with macros.

Assigning a Macro to a Toolbar

1   Select *Tools | Customise* to display the dialogue box.

2   Ensure the toolbar options are displayed by clicking on the *Toolbars* tab.

3   Scroll down the *Categories* list and highlight the *Macros* option. This will display all the available macros.

4   Click on the *QuotesBoldItalPara* macro and drag it onto the main toolbar.

5   Word prompts you to choose an icon, with the dialogue box shown in Figure 12.7.

6   Click on the icon that you want to use, then click the *Assign* button.

7   Select the *Close* button to return to the document.

8   Position the insertion point in a paragraph of text and click the new toolbar button; the macro should be executed.

*Figure 12.7.
Choosing an icon.*

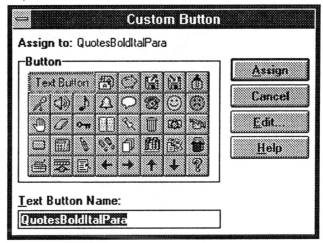

Removing a Toolbar Button

If you need to remove a button from a toolbar (either a macro button or a standard button) then you will need to use the Customise dialogue box in a similar way.

1   Select *Tools | Customise* to display the dialogue box.

2   Ensure the toolbar options are displayed by clicking on the *Toolbars* tab.

3   Click on the button on the toolbar and do one of the following:

- To remove the button altogether, drag it away from the toolbar.

- To move the button to a new location, drag it to its new location on the same or different toolbar.

Resetting a Toolbar

To reset a toolbar to its original button configuration and layout, choose the *View | Toolbars* option. The dialogue box, shown in Figure 12.8, allows all or any of the toolbars to be reset. These options also allow you to create and manage your own custom toolbars, as well as hiding or displaying any of the standard toolbars.

*Figure 12.8.
The Toolbars
dialogue box.*

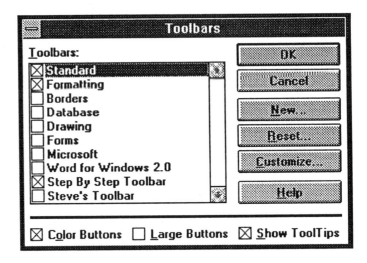

Using Keyboard Shortcuts

As with most other features of Word, keyboard shortcuts can be assigned to macros. When choosing keystroke combinations it is important to try and ensure that the shortcuts that you want to use are not currently assigned to standard Word features. If they are, and you re-assign them to a macro, then they will obviously no longer activate the original feature.

The process for assigning a shortcut is as follows:

1   Select *Tools | Customise* to display the Customise dialogue box.

2   Click on the *Keyboard* tab to display the keystroke options.

3   Select the *Macros* entry in the *Categories* list and highlight the macro that you want to assign the shortcut to.

4   Click in the *Press New Shortcut Key* box, and press the key combination that you want to use.

5   When you release the keys, a description is produced beneath the shortcut key box showing the current assignment for that combination, if any.

6   If you are satisfied with the defined combination then click on the *Assign* button.

7   Select *Close* to return to the document.

8   Position the insertion point and press the key combination to run the macro.

Exercise

1   Record or write a macro to insert a table at the current insertion point. The table should have 4 columns and 6 rows. The first row should contain headings of **London**, **Paris**, **Rome** and **Total**, and these should be emboldened and centred. Add a button to the standard toolbar to run the macro, and also define a shortcut key combination of CTRL+SHIFT+F1.

Summary

This chapter has served only as an introduction to the powerful area of macros in Word. However, by the time you have reached this part of the book you should be thinking about writing simple macros to automate repetitive operations and to customise toolbars to better reflect the tasks you want to perform.

Self Test

1   What are the limitations on the macro name?

2   How can you tell if the name given to a macro is acceptable?

3   How can you delete a macro?

4   How can you obtain help on a macro command or statement?

5   If you write or record a macro, is it available to the current document only or to other documents as well?

6   Would you need to record or write a macro if you wanted to place a button on the standard toolbar that inserted the current date into your document?

7   Is there a limit on the number of buttons that can be placed onto a toolbar?

8   How do you create a new toolbar called "Special Features"?

9   What is the easiest way to add an option to the Tools menu that runs a macro?

10   Is it possible to cause a macro to be executed automatically every time I create a new document based upon a particular template?

APPENDIX A
Answers to Self Tests

Chapter One

1 What is the name of the suite of programs that includes Microsoft Word, Excel and PowerPoint?

The suite of programs is known as Microsoft Office, and is available in two versions. Microsoft Office Standard includes Word, Excel, PowerPoint and a licence to use Mail on the workstation. Microsoft Office Professional includes all of these plus Microsoft Access, one of the most powerful and flexible database system for Windows.

2 How does version 6 of Word for Windows differ from version 6 of Word for the Macintosh?

Word 6 is almost exactly the same on the Macintosh and in Windows. Features such as formatting capabilities, graphics support, macros, wizards, templates and file formats are the same between the two. The only notable difference is a slight change to the appearance between the two, due to the differences in appearance between the Macintosh and Windows environments.

3 What does Intellisense do?

Intellisense, or AutoCorrect, is designed to correct any simple mistakes that you make whilst typing. By default it will correct mistakes involving capitalisation, quotes, and some spelling errors. In addition it can be fully customised in many different ways.

4 How much memory is needed in the PC to run Word, and how much more is recommended?

The minimum memory configuration for Word is 4MB, although more is recommended, ideally a minimum of 8MB. If you are likely to be working with complex documents, containing DDE links or OLE objects then you may find that better performance is obtained with still more memory, up to 16MB in some cases.

5 Which versions of DOS and Windows are required to run Word?

Word requires DOS version 3.1 or higher, and requires Windows version 3.1 or higher. Both of these are minimums, and you may find advantages to using more modern versions such as DOS 6.2 and Windows 3.11.

6 What is the maximum length of a DOS filename?

A DOS filename is limited in length to 8 characters, with an optional 3 character extension. However, the extension is usually reserved for use by the application, so that it can identify its own data files.

7 Which of the following filenames are valid?
                REPORT.DOC
                NEW DATA.DOC
                INFORMATION

REPORT.DOC is a valid filename as the first part of the name is only 6 characters, and the 3 character extension correctly identifies the file as a Word document.

NEW DATA.DOC is invalid as it contains a space, even though the total number of characters is within limits. Therefore this would be rejected by the software.

INFORMATION is also invalid as the name is too long. This could be made into a valid name by separating the name into an 8 character section and a 3 character section – INFORMAT.ION. However, this is likely to cause problems as your application may not automatically recognise this file and therefore this approach is not recommended.

8   How do you start Windows?

Once installed, Windows is executed by typing WIN at the DOS prompt. If this appears not to work then you may need to check the PATH statement for DOS to ensure that Windows is correctly set up. More information on this is provided in the Windows and DOS documentation.

9   What is an icon?

An icon is a small graphical image that is used to represent an application, a data file, a directory, or some special program feature in the Windows environment. Icons are a key part of any graphical user interface.

10   How do you run an application from within Windows?

To run an application you must first find its icon. This may be displayed on screen, or may be contained in one of the minimised program groups. Having located the icon, double-click it using the left mouse button to run the program. You can also use the *File | Run* command to run an application if you know the name of the program and its location on the disk.

Chapter Two

1   With Windows running, what is required to load Word for Windows?

Word is loaded by double-clicking the left mouse button whilst it is pointing to the Word Icon on the desktop. It may be necessary to first access the group in which Word is located - for example, Microsoft Office, by double-clicking on that icon first to display the window that contains the Word icon.

2   Which toolbars are displayed by default when Word is started?

Word displays the Standard toolbar and the Formatting toolbar by default. The buttons on these toolbars can be customised to suit your own requirements and you can choose to display different toolbars when you start up Word.

3   Describe two ways of displaying the Borders toolbar.

On the Formatting toolbar there is a Borders button ⊞. Clicking once on this button will display the Borders toolbar below the Formatting toolbar. Alternatively the *View | Toolbars* command may be used to check the Borders box. A third way of displaying this toolbar is to click the right mouse button with the mouse pointer somewhere on the toolbars. This will produce a list of toolbars and the Borders option may be selected.

4   What is required to make the Borders toolbar "float"?

The mouse pointer is positioned somewhere on the toolbar, but not actually on a button. You can now click and drag the toolbar to another location on the screen. You can also resize the toolbar to different shape if necessary.

5   What is required to re-anchor the Borders toolbar?

Double-clicking on the Borders toolbar title returns it to a fixed position, below the Formatting toolbar.

6   Describe two ways of hiding the Borders toolbar.

The *Borders* button on the Formatting toolbar is a *toggle* button which means that clicking on it once will display the toolbar and clicking on it again will hide the toolbar. Alternatively the *View | Toolbars* command may be used to clear the Borders box. A third way of hiding this toolbar is to click on the right mouse button with the mouse pointer somewhere on the toolbars. This will produce a list of toolbars and the Borders option may be cleared.

7   What is required to show the vertical ruler?

You must be in Page Layout View to see the vertical ruler. When in this View mode the vertical ruler will always be present providing that the Ruler option on the *View* menu has been selected.

8   What is the difference between Page 7 and 7/7 on the status bar?

Page 7 refers to the page number that will be printed for the current page, whereas 7/7 tells you the page you are on in relation to the number of pages in the document. Therefore, page 7/7 is the last page of a 7 page document.

9   What is required to turn overtype on?

Overtype can be turned on by double-clicking the *OVR* indicator at the bottom of the screen. This is a toggle feature which means that overtype can be switched off by double-clicking on the indicator again.

10   What is the effect of selecting *View* | *Full Screen*

View | *Full Screen* removes all the screen elements, replacing this space with the document. One small icon is displayed at the bottom right of the screen which, by clicking on it once, returns all the screen elements.

Chapter Three

1   What does the *insertion point* refer to ?

The insertion point is a vertical blinking bar that indicates the location in a document at which any keyboard text, graphic or clipboard item will be placed. It also indicates the place at which certain operations will begin, such as spell checking.

2   What is the difference between the DEL key and the BACKSPACE keys?

The DEL key deletes the character to the right of the insertion point and the BACKSPACE key deletes the character to the left of the insertion point.

3   Suggest two ways of saving a document for the first time.

Selecting *File* | *Save* accesses the Save dialogue box from which a file can be saved onto disk. Alternatively the *Save* button on the Standard toolbar can be used to access the same dialogue box. A third option is to select *File* | *Close* which will display a message asking whether you want to save the document before closing. Answering Yes will then access the Save dialogue box.

4   What is the quickest way to save a document using the same filename after making some changes to it?

Providing a document has been saved once, Clicking on the *Save* button on the Standard toolbar will save the current document using the existing name without the need to complete a dialogue box.

5   What problems might the use of the *fast save* cause?

Fast save only saves the changes that have been made to a document since the previous save operation. If your system crashes - either because of Word or Windows - you might not have a complete document on disk. Furthermore, Fast Save should never be used when working with Word across a network.

6   How can you change the number of files listed in the File menu?

Selecting *Tools | Options* and the *General* tab allows you to specify under the *Recently Used Files List* option the number of files you require. By default four files will be listed.

7   How is a paragraph defined in Word?

A paragraph is any amount of text or graphics that precedes a paragraph mark - ¶. A paragraph is created by pressing the ENTER key which produces an end of paragraph mark and moves the insertion point to the next line.

8   Suggest two ways of selecting a paragraph of text.

A paragraph can be selected either by triple-clicking anywhere on the paragraph, or by clicking to the left of the paragraph once the mouse pointer has changed to an arrow shape.

9   Which buttons are used to copy text from one place to another in a document?

The *Copy* button 🗐 is used to copy selected text onto the Clipboard and the Paste button 🗐 to paste a copy of that text at the insertion point.

10   How do you add a word to the AutoCorrect list?

Selecting *Tools | AutoCorrect* displays the AutoCorrect dialogue box. You can then fill in the *Replace* box with the abbreviation or incorrectly spelled word and the *With* box with the expanded abbreviation or correct spelling.

Chapter Four

1   What is the shortcut key to put text in italics whilst typing?

Pressing CTRL+I will switch on italic text whilst you are typing and pressing CTRL+I again will cancel the italics.

2   What determines the range of fonts available for your use in Word?

The number of fonts available is determined when Windows is installed and may also be affected by certain other Windows applications such as Microsoft PowerPoint and CorelDRAW!

3   What is required to put all the words in a paragraph in upper case?

The paragraph to be affected must be highlighted, either by triple-clicking on it or by clicking to the left of it and then selecting *Format | Change Case* allows you to click on the UPPERCASE option.

4   What does the tOGGLE cASE option on the Change Case dialogue box do?

Toggle case reverses the way selected text is currently displayed. For example applying the tOGGLE cASE option to the phrase 'His name is George BURTON' would produce 'hIS NAME IS gEORGE burton'.

5   What is the purpose of the *Format Painter* button on the Standard toolbar?

The *Format Painter* button allows you to copy a format to another selected piece of text. To use the feature you first format some text, then select this text and click on the *Format Painter* button. The mouse pointer changes to resemble a paintbrush and you select some further text that will automatically be formatted in the same way as the original.

6   What is the significance of the paragraph mark and where is it located?

The paragraph mark is always positioned at the end of a paragraph and it contains all the formatting that has been applied to the text or graphics preceding it.

7   Suggest two ways of seeing the formatting applied to a paragraph.

Selecting *Format | Paragraph* will produce a dialogue box with all the current formats for the highlighted paragraph, or the one in which the insertion point is positioned. Alternatively clicking on the *Help* button and then on a paragraph will display information about the formatting of that paragraph.

8   By how much is a paragraph indented when the Indent button is pressed?

The highlighted paragraph, or the one in which the insertion point is located, will be indented by one tab stop, which by default is half an inch, each time the indent button is pressed.

9   What is the difference between the square and the upward facing triangle to the left of the horizontal ruler?

The square to the left of the horizontal ruler is the paragraph indent marker and this controls the position of the left edge of the entire paragraph. The upward facing triangle only controls the position of the left edge of the first line of a paragraph.

10   How can you adjust the spacing between the text and an accompanying border?

Selecting *Format | Borders and Shading* and completing the *From Text* box specifies the amount of space left between the text and each border.

Chapter Five

1   From what point does spell checking commence?

Spell checking commences from the location of the insertion point. The only exception to this is if you select a piece of text, then checking commences at the beginning of the selection.

2 How do you begin a spelling check?

There are two ways to start the spell checker, either by clicking on the *Spelling* button on the Standard toolbar, or by selecting *Tools | Spelling*.

3 When is the Spelling dialogue box first displayed?

The Spelling dialogue box is only displayed once an unrecognised word has been found.

4 What is the difference between the *Ignore* and the *Ignore All* buttons on the Spelling dialogue box?

The *Ignore* option only ignores the current occasion of the unrecognised word, whereas *Ignore All* ignores the word until you leave Word.

5 What does the *Reset Ignore All* button on the Spelling Options dialogue box do?

If you want to re-introduce words for checking that you had previously said *Ignore All* to, the *Reset Ignore All* button will do this.

6 What file extension does a dictionary file have?

Dictionaries are standard text files, but are given a file extension of .DIC by Word.

7 What is a 'rule group' when referring to the Grammar checker?

Word has defined three rule groups which refer to different ways in which the Grammar Checker analyses a document. The options are *formal, business* and *casual*. You can, in addition specify your own customised rule groups.

8 How do you specify the required 'rule group'.

The required rule group is specified by selecting *Tools | Options* followed by the *Grammar* tab.

9   What does the *Look Up* button on the Thesaurus dialogue box do?

The *Look Up* option looks up the highlighted word in the *Meanings* list to produce another list of *Replace* options.

10   What is the difference between a nonbreaking hyphen and an optional hyphen?

A nonbrcaking hyphen prevents a hyphenated word from being split across two lines, whereas an optional hyphen allows you to specify where a hyphen should be positioned if the word is to be split across two lines.

Chapter Six

1   Suggest two ways of printing the entire document.

Providing you do not need to change any of the print specifications you can print a document by clicking on the *Print* button on the Standard toolbar. Alternatively you can select *File | Print* .

2   What is required to print pages 2 and 6 of a document?

You must access the Print dialogue box with *File | Print* and from within there you can click on the *Pages* button and then enter **2,6** to indicated that only pages 2 and 6 are required.

3   How can you print one paragraph of a document?

Select the paragraph and then click on the *Print* button which will print only the selected range.

4   What is the quickest way to access Print Preview?

Clicking on the *Print Preview* button is the quickest way to access Print Preview.

5   What is the purpose of the ALT key when adjusting margins?

Holding down the ALT key whilst adjust margins shows the actual margin dimensions as you drag the marker.

6 What is required to view six pages of a document?

Whilst in Print Preview click on the *Multiple Pages* button on the Print Preview toolbar and drag to highlight six pages. When you release the mouse button those pages will be displayed.

7 How can you shrink a document to fit on fewer pages from within Print Preview?

Click on the *Shrink to Fit* button on the Print Preview toolbar and the system will attempt to reduce the number of pages in the document by one page.

8 Having viewed multiple pages how can you return to a single page?

Click on the *One Page* button will return Print Preview to displaying only the page on which the insertion point is currently located.

9 How do you change the percentage size of the document on the screen from within Print Preview?

On the Print Preview toolbar there is a percentage box into which you can type the percentage size you want to view or you can use the up and down arrows to the right of the box to select the required size.

10 How can you edit the document while in Print Preview?

Display the page you want to edit and click on the part of the page you want to be in. As you move onto the text the mouse pointer changes to a magnifying glass and when you click once that part of the screen is magnified. Clicking on the *Magnify* button on the toolbar changes the pointer to an I-beam and editing may be performed. To return to the display prior to editing click on the *Magnify* button again.

Chapter Seven

1 How can you see the styles supplied by Word?

Holding the SHIFT key whilst clicking the arrow to the right of the Style box on the Formatting toolbar will display the full list of available character and paragraph styles.

2   What is the difference between a character style and a paragraph style?

A character style allows you to select any piece of text and apply a predefined set of formats on it, whereas a paragraph style automatically applies the predefined formats on an entire paragraph or series of paragraphs.

3   How do you identify a Character style from the list in the Style box?

Character styles are not displayed in bold, whereas paragraph styles are.

4   What does the F4 function key do?

This function key repeats the last operation you performed. It is useful in the style context in that you can create a character style which you apply to some text, then selecting another piece of text and pressing F4 will format that text with the same style.

5   How can you return text formatted with a character style to the Default Paragraph Font?

You can either press CTRL+SPACEBAR to return selected text to the Default Paragraph Font, or you can select the Default Paragraph Font from the Style box.

6   How do you assign a shortcut key to an existing paragraph style?

Select *Format* | *Style* and click on the style you want to assign a shortcut key to. Click on the *Modify* button followed by the *Shortcut Key* button. With the insertion point to the *Press New Shortcut Key* box, press the key combination you want to use. Click the *Assign* button and close the dialogue boxes to return to the document.

7   What is the shortcut key combination to return a paragraph style to Normal?

Pressing CTRL+SHIFT+N will return a selected paragraph to Normal style.

8   What effect does redefining a paragraph style have on the rest of the document?

When you change the formatting of a paragraph, only that paragraph is affected. However, if you redefine the paragraph style, all the paragraphs in the document will be redefined with the new formatting.

9   How do you access the AutoFormat command?

Selecting *Format | AutoFormat* access the AutoFormat dialogue box.

10   What do you have to do to apply styles from a different template when using AutoFormat?

The Style Gallery option on the AutoFormat dialogue box allows you to select styles to be used in the current document from other templates.

Chapter Eight

1   What file extension is given by Word to a wizard file?

Wizard files are assigned a file extension of .WIZ by Word.

2   Which view mode should you be in when using a wizard?

You should be in Normal View before loading a Wizard.

3   What does a small square to the left of a paragraph mean?

This small square indicates that the paragraph cannot be split across two pages. Although this is a feature regularly seen in Wizard files, you can specify it yourself in the *Format | Paragraph* dialogue box by clicking on the *Text Flow* tab and checking the *Keep With Next* box.

4   What is the main difference between a wizard and a template?

Wizards prompt you to fill out the formatting specifications for a document on a step by step basis, whereas a template file gives you a fully formatted boilerplate for your document, the entries for which you fill in with your own information.

5   What file extension is given by Word to a template file?

Template files are assigned the extension of .DOT

6   Where are template files normally found?

By default Word will always expect to find template files in the \WINWORD\TEMPLATES directory.

7   When you have customised a template what save command must you use and why?

It is important that you use the *File | Save As* command to save a template file that you have customised with a different name. Using the *Save* button or the *File Save* command will overwrite the original template with the customised template.

8   How can you change the location of a template file?

Selecting *Tools | Options* and the *File Locations* tab enables to you change the path that Word searches for template files.

9   How can you obtain a description of a template?

Selecting *File | New* and clicking on one of the listed template files will display a brief description in the *Description* box at the bottom of the dialogue box.

10   What template will be used if you start a new document by clicking on the *New* button on the Standard Toolbar?

The NORMAL.DOT template is used when the *New* button is clicked to start a new document.

Chapter Nine

1   How do you format an existing document to be across three columns?

Click on the *Column* button on the Standard toolbar and drag the mouse pointer across three columns. When you release the mouse button the document will be formatted across three columns. Note that you will only see the full effect of this if you are in Page Layout view.

2 What must you do if you want the document title to be centred between the document margins?

The document title must be in a different section to the text in multiple columns. Therefore before creating columns, insert a continuous section break with the *Insert |Break* command immediately after the document title and then format the second section with multiple columns. The title can be centred with the *Centre* button on the Formatting toolbar.

3 How do you draw a vertical line between two columns?

Check the *Line Between* box on the Column dialogue box which is accessed by selecting *Format | Columns*.

4 What command is required to change the formatting of a paragraph to two columns in an otherwise one column document?

Insert a continuous section break immediately before and after the paragraph to be formatted to two columns. Then, with the insertion point somewhere on the paragraph to be formatted, use the *Column* button to specify two columns.

5 How do you ensure that columns are balanced?

Inserting a section break at the end of the text in columns ensures they are balanced. You should do this at the end of a document if multiple columns are in use at that point.

6 How can you change the margins for a particular section?

Selecting *File | Page Setup* allows you to specify top and bottom, left and right margins. In a document with multiple sections the *Apply To* box has an option to apply the settings only to the current section, as opposed to the entire document.

7   On which toolbar is the Table button?

The *Table* button is located on the Standard toolbar.

8   How do you move across a row from cell to cell when entering text?

The TAB key is used to move from cell to cell across a row in a table.

9   How do you insert an additional row at the bottom of a table?

With the insertion point in the bottom right cell of the table, pressing TAB will insert a new line at the bottom of the table.

10   How do you centre a table between the document margins?

Select the entire table with *Table | Select Table* and then select *Table | Cell Height and Width*. Click on the Row tab and then click on the *Center* button in the Alignment section. Click *OK* to return to the document.

Chapter Ten

1   How many graphic file formats can Word recognise?

Word can recognise up to 8 specifically named graphic file formats: DrawPerfect, Micrografx Designer/Draw, Computer Graphics Metafile (CGM), Encapsulated PostScript (EPS), Tag Image File Format (TIFF), Macintosh PICT, PCX, and Compuserve GIF.

2   What command is used to insert a picture into a Word document?

To insert a picture that is held in a file on the disk, the *Insert | Picture* command is used. It is also possible to use the Clipboard, DDE or OLE techniques to insert a picture that has been generated in another Windows application.

3   How can you preview a picture prior to inserting it into a document?

Having selected the *Insert | Picture* command, the resulting dialogue box will be found to contain a *Preview Picture* option in the lower right hand corner; if this is checked then each time you click on a different picture file in the file list, the image will be previewed on-screen.

4 Which directory does Word store the provided clipart in?

When Word is installed, all clipart is placed into a subdirectory of the main WINWORD directory called CLIPART. If required this can be changed by choosing *Tools | Options* and selecting the *File Locations* tab. These options allow the locations of the different file types that Word uses to be changed.

5 What is the difference between using a corner handle and a side handle when resizing a picture?

Sizing a picture using a corner handle will maintain the *aspect ratio* – the width to height proportion of the picture. This means that no matter what size the picture is, it looks like the original. Sizing a picture using an edge handle (at the left, right, top or bottom) allows it to be stretched in one direction, thereby changing the original proportions. This can be used to create some interesting special effects.

6 What is the effect of the *Link To File* command?

The standard *Insert | Picture* causes a one-off copy of the picture to be inserted into the current document; even if the file on disk changes the document will remain unchanged. By selecting the *Link To File* option you can ensure that any such modifications to the picture are reflected automatically in your document.

7 What does DDE stand for and what is the benefit of using this technique?

DDE stands for Dynamic Data Exchange, and provides a way of establishing a general-purpose link between two Windows applications. Having transferred data from one application to another using DDE, this approach ensures that any changes made in the source application (the one providing the original data) are also made in the destination application (the one receiving the data).

8   When working with a DDE link, what is the difference between a *manual* and an *automatic* link?

A manual link requires that you select the ***Edit | Links*** command and choose the *Update* button if you want your document to reflect any changes that may have been made to the source data. An automatic link requires no such user interaction as it will ensure that any changes made to the source data are immediately reflected in the destination.

9   What does OLE stand for and how does it differ from DDE?

OLE stands for Object Linking and Embedding, and appears to offer a very similar set of features to DDE. In fact OLE can be thought of as a more elegant form of DDE, offering not only the ability to link (which works the same as for DDE) but also the ability to embed data (which creates a complete, editable copy of the information in your document).

10   How do you edit an image that has been inserted into a document as an OLE object?

Any OLE object can be edited by double-clicking it. This causes the original application to be executed, and the OLE data to be loaded ready for changes to be made.

Chapter Eleven

1   From which menu will you find the Mail Merge option?

Mail Merge is part of the ***Tools*** menu.

2   What must you create first in the Mail Merge process?

You must create, at least an outline for, the main document into which your variable information will be placed. You are prompted to do this on selecting ***Tools | Mail Merge*** which launches the Mail Merge Helper. This feature guides you through the necessary steps in the order you are advised to work in. You do not need to type the body of the main document at this stage.

3   What is the difference between a data record and a data field?

A data *record* consists of all the information about a particular item. For example, the name, job title, company, address, telephone number, for an individual constitutes one record. Any item within that record, for example the individual's name, is a data *field*. Therefore a group of data fields form a data record, and a group of data records form a data *file*.

4   What are the rules for field names in the Data Source file?

A field name may consist of up to 40 characters. A name must start with a letter, and subsequent characters must be letters, numbers, or the underscore (_). No spaces are allowed.

5   How do you change the position of a field in a data record?

In the Create Data Source dialogue box there are two arrows to the right of the Field names list which allow you to *move* the position of fields. You must first click on the field you wish to move to select it and then use the up or down arrow to reposition it.

6   How can you add a new field into a data record?

In the Create Data Source dialogue box type a new field name into the *Field Name* box, then click on the *Add Field Name* box which will place the new name at the end of the list. You can then reposition it to the required location.

7   How can you move back to a field in the data form to make a correction?

When entering data into a data form you can move the insertion point up to previous fields by pressing SHIFT+TAB.

8   What button is used to insert a merge field into the main document?

The *Insert Merge Field* button on the Mail Merge toolbar inserts a merge field into the main document at the position the insertion point is located.

9   What does the *Merge to Printer* button on the Mail Merge toolbar do?

The *Merge To Printer* button merges the Data Source file with the Main Document directly to the printer, as opposed to creating a new document.

10   How is each letter separated if a data file is merged to a new document?

A section break is automatically inserted at the end of each letter when a new document is created.

Chapter Twelve

1   What are the limitations on the macro name?

The macro name can be no more than 36 characters long, and must not contain spaces, commas or periods.

2   How can you tell if the name given to a macro is acceptable?

As you enter the name into the Macro dialogue box the *Create* button will be greyed out if the name is not acceptable. If you are using the Record Macro dialogue box, the *OK* button is greyed out for unacceptable names.

3   How can you delete a macro?

To delete a macro select the *Tools | Macro* commands, highlight the name of the macro to be deleted, then click the *Delete* button. You will prompted to confirm that you wish to delete the macro before it is erased.

4   How can you obtain help on a macro command or statement?

Help in Word is context-sensitive, which means that if you select something then activate help, you will receive information on whatever was activated. Therefore to obtain help on any macro command, position the insertion point somewhere in the command and press F1.

5 If you write or record a macro, is it available to the current document only or to other documents as well?

Each macro that is created is available to all documents based on the template that contains the macro. Therefore if the macro is created in the NORMAL.DOT template it will be available to all documents, but if it is placed within a specific template, such as INVOICE.DOT, it is available only to documents based upon INVOICE.DOT.

6 Would you need to record or write a macro if you wanted to place a button on the standard toolbar that inserted the current date into your document?

It is not necessary to use a macro to insert the current date as there is a command available that does this for you. A button could be added to a toolbar to represent this command by choosing *Tools | Customize*, selecting the *Toolbars* tab and changing the *Category* to *All Commands*. Select *InsertDateTime* in the *Command* list and drag it onto a toolbar. Choose an appropriate button when prompted, then select *Close* to return to the document. Clicking the new button will then produce the standard Date and Time dialogue box.

7 Is there a limit on the number of buttons that can be placed onto a toolbar?

The number of buttons that can be placed onto a toolbar is effectively limited by the displayed size of the toolbar. If it is docked then the toolbar can only show as many buttons as will fit in the width or height of the screen. If the toolbar is floating then more buttons will be visible.

8 How do you create a new toolbar called "Special Features"?

Select *View | Toolbars* then click the *New* button. You will be prompted for the toolbar name, which should be entered as **Special Features**, and where the toolbar will be stored (NORMAL.DOT by default). On clicking OK the toolbar customisation dialogue box is displayed, allowing you to place buttons onto the new toolbar.

9   What is the easiest way to add an option to the Tools menu that runs a macro?

Menus can be customised in the same way as toolbars and keyboard shortcuts, so to add a command to run a macro the following is required. Select **Tools | Customize** and select the *Menus* tab. Select the *Macros* option in the *Categories* list, click on the name of the macro to be added in the *Macros* list and choose the *Add* button. Select the *Close* button to return to the document and you will find that the macro has been added to the *Tools* menu. Other options in the Customize dialogue box allow the position of the macro on the menu to be controlled.

10   Is it possible to cause a macro to be executed automatically every time I create a new document based upon a particular template?

Certain macro names have special effects in Word and allow you to produce effects such as the above. In this case the macro would need to be named AutoNew, and would be stored in the appropriate template. Each time a new document is created from this template the macro is executed automatically. Other "auto" macro names include AutoExec, AutoOpen, AutoClose and AutoExit.

APPENDIX B
Example Files

Introduction

The following pages contain complete printed copies of the files used in the step-by-step examples and exercises throughout this book.

ALICE_A.DOC

This file is used in Chapters Three, Four, Six, Ten and Twelve.

One thing was for certain, that the white kitten had had nothing to do with it - it was the black kitten's fault entirely. For the white kitten had been having its face washed by the old cat for the last quarter of an hour (and bearing it pretty well, considering): so you see that it couldn't have had any hand in the mischief.

The way Dinah washed her children's faces was this; first she held the poor thing down by its ear with one paw, and then with the other paw she rubbed its face all over, the wrong way, beginning at the nose: and just now, as I said, she was hard at work on the white kitten, which was lying quite still and trying to purr - no doubt feeling that it was all meant for its good.

PROOF_A.DOC and COLUMN_A.DOC

This file is used as PROOF_A in Chapter Five for spell checking and so deliberately contains a number of typographical errors. In order that you can enter these into the document, you will need to turn off AutoCorrect by selecting **Tools | AutoCorrect** and clearing the *Replace Text as you Type* option.

A correct version of the file is used as COLUMN_A.DOC in Chapter Nine.

CHINA - THE GEOGRAPHY AND HISTORY

It is 2500 miles from Shanghai on China's eastern seaboard to Kashgar on its far western frontier. Only about 12 percent of this vast land can be cultivated and most of that is in the east adjacent to the seaboard where 95 percent of China's nearly one billion people now live. The western half is divided between the remote Tibetan highlands nad the deserts and steppes of Inner Mongolia.

China's civilisation began in the valley of the Yellow River, the northernmost of her three great eastward floowing rivers. The Yangtze River, which meats the see near Shanghai, deevides south China form the North China Plain. In the mountainous south the West River draws on many tributaries in its path to the the sea near Canton. In the north the main crops are millet, maize and wheat. The great rice growing andsilk producing areas lie in the Yangtze Valley and the south, whose mountain slopes also produce the teas for which China is famous.

Over most of China a standard form of Chinese derived from Northern Mandarin is now spoken. In the southern provinces the people also maintain their own distinctive dialects, such as Cantonese, with a pronunciation so different and a tonal pattern so complex that they are unintelligible to their compatriots in the north. The southwestern provinces are the home of numerous minority peoples and all maintain their own distinctive ways of life.

Remains of early man in China going back to 700,000 BC have been found to the south of Peking, where Peking Man was discovered, and which was occupied from about 500,000 BC. Early Chinese civilisation grew up along the fertile Yellow river valley, and by 4000 BC communities they were living in neolithic villages similar to the ones preserved in museums. Here they farmed and hunted and painted their pottery with geometric designs. To the east another group of people grew rice and made find black pottery on the wheel.

Piece compiled by Professor H Stendalton

STYLE_A.DOC

This file is used in Chapter Seven.

MASTERING WINDOWS

Introduction

The definitive course to discover how you can get the most out of the *Windows* operating environment

Windows and Windows applications are now firmly accepted as leaders in the personal computer market. But many users are only exploiting a fraction of the power that can be derived from this sophisticated working environment.

This two day course has been designed to explain and illustrate how to maximise the potential of your Windows systems, both in terms of optimising the installation of Windows itself as well as looking at the key features of some popular Windows applications.

The sessions will concentrate on the power usage of applications rather than 'sales like' demonstrations. Using realistic business examples participants will learn how DDE and OLE can revolutionise PC usage. The use of multi-media and sound through Windows will also be shown.

The seminar leaders will give up to the minute information and advice about the different operating platforms available to run Windows and the course will include a comparison between Windows 3.1, Windows NT, Windows for Workgroups and all their main competitors.

The specific implications of running Windows over a network will be addressed, both in terms of technical benefits and problems that can occur as well as from the user perspective.

What You Will Learn

- To show how Windows can be optimised for maximum performance
- To demonstrate the power features of major Windows applications
- To show how data can be linked across applications through the use of DDE and OLE
- To demonstrate current innovations and to look at what is in store for Windows users in the future.

Course Documentation

A comprehensive workbook containing many useful hints, tips and worked examples will be supplied to all participants. This will be invaluable for reference after the course. Additionally a disk containing sample macro, spreadsheet, document and other files will be provided.

SALES_A.DOC

This file is used in Chapter Nine.

REGIONAL SALES SUMMARY

The regions have all performed well this month with sales up by a minimum of 10% in all cases. The table below show's each department's sales for last month and for this month.

I would like you to consider likely targets for next month and have them ready for discussion at the next sales meeting to be held on Friday at 15.00.

MAIN_A.DOC

This file is used in Chapter Eleven.

---

28 April 1994

«Title» «FirstName» «LastName»
«JobTitle»
«Company»
«Address1»
«Address2»
«City»
«PostalCode»
«County»

Dear «Title» «LastName»

Thank you for attending our Marketing Skills training course last week. I enclose your certificate and am pleased to tell you that you gained a mark of «Results»

The next course we will be running in the «City» area will be in August.

Yours sincerely,

Michael Watson

DATA.DOC

This file is created in Chapter Eleven, but the data has been reproduced here in its entirety for easier reference.

Title	Mrs	Mr	Ms
FirstName	Diane	Henry	Sally
LastName	King	Jinks	Ellis
JobTitle	Marketing Manager	Marketing Assistant	Director
Company	Grosvenor Cutlery	Beds Galore	Sally's Curtains
Address1	45 Gregson Place	4 High Street	2 Coopers Lane
Address2	Central Business Park	Little Marsham	
City	Gloucester	Oxford	Redhill
County	GLOS	OXON	Surrey
PostalCode	G34 6HP	OX3 4PK	RH4 7DF
Results	80%	75%	90%

Index

D